Identity Economics

A new cadet (on left) entering West Point salutes the cadet in the Red Sash (on right) in his company. During Reception Day, the new cadets begin the process of becoming United States Army officers. They undergo administrative processing, are fitted with their initial issue of military clothing, have their hair cut, and start their first lessons in marching, military manners, and discipline.

http://www.westpoint.edu

Identity Economics

HOW OUR IDENTITIES SHAPE OUR
WORK, WAGES, AND WELL-BEING

GEORGE A. AKERLOF
AND
RACHEL E. KRANTON

Princeton University Press • PRINCETON AND OXFORD

Published by Princeton University Press, 41 William Street,
Princeton, New Jersey 08540

In the United Kingdom: Princeton University Press,
6 Oxford Street, Woodstock, Oxfordshire OX20 1TW

Library of Congress Cataloging-in-Publication Data

Akerlof, George A., 1940–
    Identity economics : how our identities shape our work, wages, and
well-being / George A. Akerlof and Rachel E. Kranton.
        p.   cm.
    Includes bibliographical references and index.
    ISBN 978-0-691-14648-5 (hbk. : alk. paper)
    1. Economics—Psychological aspects.   2. Identity (Psychology).
3. Economics—Social aspects.   I. Kranton, Rachel E.   II. Title.
    HB74.P8A4944   2010
    306.3—dc22   2009038216

British Library Cataloging-in-Publication Data is available

This book has been composed in New Baskerville and Syntax by
Princeton Editorial Associates, Inc., Scottsdale, Arizona

Printed on acid-free paper. ∞

press.princeton.edu

Printed in the United States of America

10 9 8 7 6

Contents

CONTENTS

Part Four: Looking Ahead

Part One

Economics and Identity

ONE

Introduction

ANN HOPKINS WAS HIRED in Price Waterhouse's Office of Government Services in 1978. By all accounts, she was hardworking and diligent. She retrieved from the discard pile a State Department request for proposals and masterminded it into a contract worth approximately $25 million.[1] It was the largest consulting contract Price Waterhouse had ever secured, and her clients at the State Department raved about her work. In 1982 she was put up for partner, the lone woman among eighty-eight candidates.[2] But the promotion did not go through.

What was deemed wrong with her performance? Colleagues complained about her deportment and the way she treated her staff. In their written comments on her promotion, the senior partners observed: "Needs a course in charm school," "macho," and "overcompensated for being a woman." Her boss, who supported her, told her that if she wanted to make partner she should "walk more femininely, talk more femininely, dress more femininely, wear makeup and jewelry, and have her hair styled."[3]

Hopkins sued, on the grounds of sex discrimination under Title VII of the Civil Rights Act. After a series of appeals, the case reached the U.S. Supreme Court in 1988. There, the majority held that the firm had applied a double standard. The court wrote that "an employer who objects to aggressiveness in women but whose positions require this trait places women in an intolerable and impermissible catch 22: out of a job if they behave aggressively, and out of a job if they do not."[4]

Price Waterhouse v. Hopkins is an illustration of identity economics at work. The partners were applying contemporary norms for behavior: *men* were supposed to behave one way, *women* another. We could interpret these views as reflecting basic tastes or preferences—they just liked working with women who talked and walked "more femininely." But these are not basic tastes such as "I like bananas" and "You like oranges," which are the foundations of the economic theory of trade. Rather, these tastes depend on the social setting and who is interacting with whom. The tastes derive from *norms,* which we define as the social rules regarding how people *should* behave in different situations. These rules are sometimes explicit, sometimes implicit, largely internalized, and often deeply held. And the "preferences" or "tastes" that derive from these norms are frequently the subject of dispute, so much so that—as in *Hopkins*—they may even be adjudicated in court.

This book introduces identity and related norms into economics. The discipline of economics no longer confines itself to questions about consumption and income: economists today also consider a wide variety of noneconomic motives. But identity economics brings in something new. In every social context, people have a notion of who they are, which is associated with beliefs about how they and others are supposed to behave. These notions, as we will see, play important roles in how economies work.

We begin with the *Hopkins* case because the type of identity involved—that of gender—is so obvious. Even as toddlers, children learn that boys and girls should act differently. But gender, and equally obviously race, are just the clearest manifestations of identity and norms. In this book we study norms in many different contexts—in workplaces, homes, and schools.

To see the salience of identity in economic life, let's take another example from a source where it might be least expected. On Wall Street, reputedly, the name of the game is making money. Charles Ellis's history of Goldman Sachs shows that, paradoxically, the partnership's success in making money comes from subordinating that goal, at least in the short run.[5] Rather, the company's financial success has stemmed from an ideal remarkably like that of the U.S. Air Force: "Service before Self." Employees believe, above all, that they are to serve the firm. As a managing director recently told us: "At Goldman we run to the fire." Goldman Sachs's Business Principles, fourteen of them, were composed in the 1970s by the firm's co-chairman, John Whitehead, who feared that the firm might lose its core values as it grew. The first Principle is "Our clients' interests always come first. Our experience shows that if we serve our clients well, our own success will follow." The principles also mandate dedication to teamwork, innovation, and strict adherence to rules and standards. The final principle is "Integrity and honesty are at the heart of our business. We expect our people to maintain high ethical standards in everything they do, both in their work for the firm and in their personal lives."[6] Like the military and other civilian companies we examine later in the book, Goldman Sachs is an example of identity economics in action. The employees do not act according to basic tastes: by accepting Whitehead's principles, they identify with the firm and uphold its ideals in both their professional and their personal lives. The creed is: "Absolute loyalty to the firm and to the partnership."[7]

Origins of Identity Economics

Our work on identity and economics began in 1995, when we were both, by coincidence, based in Washington, DC. We had been together at Berkeley—George as a professor, Rachel as a graduate student. George then went to the Brookings Institution while his wife was serving on the Federal Reserve Board. Rachel was at the University of Maryland.

Identity Economics began with a letter from Rachel to George telling him that his most recent paper was wrong.[8] He had ignored identity, she wrote, and this concept was also critically missing from economics more generally. We decided to meet. Quite possibly, we thought, identity was already captured in the economics of the time; perhaps it was already included in what we call *tastes*.

We talked for months. We discussed the research of sociologists, anthropologists, psychologists, political scientists, historians, and literary critics. We discussed the focus on identity: how people think they and others should behave; how society teaches them how to behave; and how people are motivated by these views, sometimes to the point of being willing to die for them. We worked to distill many ideas and nuances, to develop a basic definition of identity that could be easily incorporated into economics. And we saw that including identity would have implications for fields as disparate as macroeconomics and the economics of education.[9]

This book builds an economics where tastes vary with social context. Identity and norms bring something new to the representation of tastes. Garden-variety tastes for oranges and bananas —to continue with the earlier example—are commonly viewed as being characteristic of the individual. In contrast, identities and norms derive from the social setting. The incorporation of identity and norms then yields a theory of decision making where social context matters.

This vision of tastes is important because norms are powerful sources of motivation. Norms affect fine-grain decisions of the moment—decisions as trivial as which T-shirt we wear to go jogging. Norms drive life-changing decisions as well: on matters as important as whether to quit school, whether and whom to marry, whether to work, save, invest, retire, and fight wars. We will see throughout the book that identities and norms are easy to observe. Anthropologists and sociologists are professional observers of norms. But norms and identities are also easy to see in day-to-day life. We have already seen two examples: Goldman Sachs, with its fourteen principles, and Price Waterhouse, with the partners' descriptions of Hopkins. People express their views in the ways they describe themselves and others. As the Supreme Court put it in the *Hopkins* decision, "It takes no special training to discern sex stereotyping in a description of an aggressive female employee as requiring 'a course at charm school.' Nor does it require expertise in psychology to know that, if an employee's flawed 'interpersonal skills' can be corrected by a soft-hued suit or a new shade of lipstick, perhaps it is the employee's sex, and not her interpersonal skills, that has drawn the criticism."[10]

Until now, economists have had neither the language nor the analytical apparatus to use such evidence or to describe such norms and motivations. Of course, many economists have suggested related nonmonetary reasons for people's actions, such as morality, altruism, and concern for status. This book provides both a vocabulary and a unifying analytical framework to study such motives.

Ideas Have Consequences

Economics—for better or for worse—pervades how policy makers, the public, and the press talk and think. Modern economics follows Adam Smith's attempt in the eighteenth century to turn moral philosophy into a social science designed to create a good society. Smith enlisted all human passions and social institutions in this effort. In the nineteenth century, economists began to build mathematical models of how the economy worked, using a stick figure of a rationally optimizing human with only economic motivations. As economics evolved into the twentieth century, the models grew more sophisticated, but *Homo economicus* lagged behind. This began to change when Gary Becker developed ways to represent a variety of realistic tastes, such as for discrimination, children, and altruism.[11] Fairly recently, behavioral economics has introduced cognitive bias and other psychological findings. *Identity Economics,* in its turn, brings in social context—with a new economic man and woman who resemble real people in real situations.[12]

What does this increased humanity buy us? We get a more reliable model, which makes economics a more useful tool for improving institutions and society. This richer, socially framed conception of individual decision making should help economists working at various levels to construct sturdier accounts of the economy. Social scientists in other disciplines should find identity economics useful because it connects economic models with their own work, enabling the development of richer accounts of social processes. And policy analysts and business strategists will benefit from identity economics because it offers ways of more accurately predicting the consequences of public policies and business practices.

"Ideas have consequences" was a theme at Milton Friedman's ninetieth birthday celebration at the White House in 2002.[13] As John Maynard Keynes wrote two generations earlier: "Madmen in authority, who hear voices in the air, are distilling their frenzy from some academic scribbler of a few years back."[14] Identity economics restores human passions and social institutions into economics. Whether economics includes or excludes identity, then, also has its consequences.

TWO

Identity Economics

THIS CHAPTER INTRODUCES THE framework of identity economics. It shows the fault line between economics with and without identity and norms.

Identity, Norms, and Utility Functions

Economists have a way of describing motivation: we describe an individual as having a "utility function." This is a mathematical expression that characterizes what people care about. For example, a person may care about today's consumption and about future consumption. That person then makes decisions to maximize her utility function. For example, she will choose how much to borrow and how much to save. This mathematics may seem like a roundabout way of describing motivation, but it turns out to be useful. Utility functions and what goes into them give economists a formal way to classify motivation. In principle, a utility function can express any sort of motivation.

9

Most economic analysis concentrates on pecuniary motivations, such as desires for consumption and income. But economics today is not just about money, and many economists believe that we should study nonpecuniary motives as well. Utility functions have been developed to express a wide array of nonpecuniary tastes and preferences, such as the desire for children, the concern for status, and the desire for fairness and retribution.

But in this welter of activity, with rare exception, economists have maintained the basic presumption that such tastes and preferences are individual characteristics independent of social context. Some individuals simply care more about children, others less. Some people care more about status, others less. And so on. This presumption ignores the fact that what people care about, and how much they care about it, depends in part on their identity.

We illustrate with the example of "fairness." Leading economists, including John Nash, Hal Varian, Matthew Rabin, and Ernst Fehr, have brought fairness into our purview.[1] They argue that people care about being fair and being treated fairly. The utility function then should take account of such concerns. Fairness thus conceived can explain many results from experiments where subjects—usually students at a university laboratory—participate in scenarios that mimic economic transactions. Instead of maximizing their own monetary reward, subjects tend to choose outcomes that look "fair."[2]

But in the real world, individuals' conceptions of fairness depend on the social context. In many places it is seen as fair and perhaps natural to treat other people in ways that elsewhere are considered unfair and even cruel. This observation is as important as it is obvious. In India, upper castes do not treat lower castes equally. In Rwanda, Tutsis and Hutus do not treat each other equally. In America, whites have not treated blacks equally. We also see unfairness in daily interactions. We see it on the playground. We see it in hospital surgery rooms, in the interaction between doctors and scrub nurses. In many countries, even today, women and girls are physically assaulted; they are not permitted to go to school or leave their homes, let alone vote, own property, or open a bank account.

These examples have one thing in common: they all involve people's identities. The norms of how to behave depend on people's positions within their social context. Thus, people's tastes for fairness depend on who is interacting with whom and in what social setting. And indeed, in experiments that explicitly match people with different social identities, the subjects treat others differently. We review such experimental evidence in Chapter 4.

Social Categories, Ideals, and Observation

How do people know the norms that apply to their situation, prescribing what they and others should or should not do? We learn a great deal from watching others. An obvious example occurs in the acquisition of language, where children—effortlessly, it seems—learn to speak by copying others. Not only do they learn words and grammar, but, remarkably, they also mimic exact pronunciations. Furthermore, they make subtle distinctions when learning language.[3] Immigrant children adopt the accents of their peers, not those of their parents. Children as young as six understand that there are different styles of speech that are appropriate for talking to some people but inappropriate for talking to others. Thus, for example, Lisa Delpit tells of the black first-grader who asked her teacher, "How come you talkin' like a white person, . . . like my momma talk when she get on the phone?"[4]

In the formal language of the social sciences, people divide themselves and others into *social categories*. And social categories and norms are automatically tied together: people in different social categories *should* behave differently. The norms also specify how people of different types—different social categories, in our new vocabulary—should treat each other.

Identity, norms, and social categories may appear to be abstract concepts, but their reality is both powerful and easy to see. Norms are particularly clear when people hold an *ideal* of who they should be and how they should act. (By *ideal* we mean the exemplary characteristics and behavior associated with a social category.) This ideal may be embodied by a real or imagined person. Religions offer obvious and powerful examples. The founder of a religion and its leading prophets or saints are often exemplars. For Christians, the life of Jesus Christ, as described by the Gospels, gives an ideal of how they should behave. For Muslims, it is the life of Muhammad and the Sunnah. We also observe categories, norms, and ideals in how people talk about their lives. Many people can readily describe how they think they should behave and how others should behave. Transgressions are the stuff of gossip. The outside observer—for example, the visiting anthropologist—need only learn the stories and listen to the gossip to infer the norms.

A small slice of everyday life in America, as observed by Erving Goffman, gives an elementary example of identity and norms in action.[5] Goffman described children at a merry-go-round. Children are very aware of their age. They state their precise ages proudly, not only in years, but often in months, and sometimes even in days. Children understand norms for age-specific behavior well: they know that big kids should act differently from little kids. Children at the merry-go-round thus yield a natural experiment that shows the role of norms. We can observe how children of different ages react to the merry-go-round. Toddlers ride on their parents' laps. Four- and five-year-olds ride alone. Proud of their accomplishment, they smile and wave at their parents, who are standing on the side. Older children try to hide their excitement—they ride a funny animal, like a frog or a tiger, or they stand up while the carousel is in motion. You can see in their faces that they like the merry-go-round, but they are also embarrassed. They will act like a thirteen-year-old boy we ourselves saw last summer. He first fidgeted on a horse; then he switched to an ostrich; and then he changed animals yet again. Before the end of the ride, he had gotten off entirely.

Why do older children act this way? It is not because they dislike the merry-go-round, at least in the conventional way economists describe tastes. On the contrary, older children seem—like the younger children—to be entranced by the rotation and the music. The older children are ambivalent because they like the carousel, but they also know they should be too old for it.

Such interplay of tastes and norms lies at the heart of this book. The merry-go-round illustrates a general point. When people are doing what they think they should be doing, they are happy, like the four- and five-year-olds. But those who are not living up to the norms that they (and others) have set for themselves, like the older children, are unhappy. They then change their decisions to meet their standards.

Putting It All Together

This book incorporates *identity, norms,* and *social categories* into economics. We also use the word *identity* as shorthand to bundle together these three terms. The term *identity* has been used in many different ways in academic research and in popular usage. Many economists would say it is a fuzzy concept. We give it a precise definition in the context of our analysis. People's identity defines who they are—their social category. Their identities will influence their decisions, because different norms for behavior are associated with different social categories. Goffman's carousel is an elementary example. First, there are social categories: the different age groups of the children. Second, there are norms for how someone in those social categories should or should not behave. Third, norms affect behavior. The thirteen year-old cannot enjoy the merry-go-round; so he makes his way off.

Identity Economics and Supply and Demand

Our discussion of identity and utility has ranged from merry-go-rounds to genocide. And indeed a major point of our book is that the concepts of identity and norms, and their dependence on social category, have great versatility. Identity may describe the interactions of an instant, a day, a few years, a lifetime, or generations. For example, over the course of a day, a woman may see herself as a mother at home and a professional at work. The social category then refers to how she sees herself at the time. And over a lifetime, people can dramatically change their understanding of their lives.

Thus identity has the same kind of versatility as our tried-and-true notion of supply and demand. On the one hand, supply and demand may refer respectively to the supply and demand for a given stock or bond for just a few seconds. But it may also refer to supply and demand in the aggregate economy over long periods. In each case we refer to supply and demand in the relevant context.

We use the concept of identity similarly. In the relevant context, analysis of demand and supply leads us first to identify individuals as buyers or sellers. Second, we specify the prevailing technology and the market structure. And third, we look for individual gains and losses from particular actions such as choice of prices or purchases. Analogously, with identity, we first associate individuals with particular social categories. Second, we specify the prevailing norms for these categories. And third, we posit individual gains and losses from different decisions, given identities and corresponding norms. These gains and losses, combined with the standard concerns of economic analysis, will then determine what people do.

Outline of the Book

Part 1 of the book builds the framework of identity economics. In it, we explain how we formally bring identity and norms into economic analysis and discuss where these concepts fit into today's economics.

Parts 2 and 3 apply our framework to four substantive areas of economics. We study organizations, education, gender in the labor market and in the home, and race and poverty. In each case our approach leads to new and different conclusions. For example, it offers a new understanding of organizations. About forty years ago economists began to build a theory of work incentives, emphasizing the role of wages and bonuses. A good company, according to the theory, gets those incentives right. But a more subtle view draws a near-opposite conclusion. If employees care only about wages and bonuses, they will game the system. They will do what it takes to earn the bonus, but not necessarily what is good for the clients or for the firm. If monetary incentives alone do not work, what does? Identity economics suggests that a firm operates well when employees identify with it and when their norms advance its goals. Because firms and other organizations are the backbone of all economies, this new description transforms our understanding of what makes economies work or fail.

Looking inside schools, we also have a new understanding of education. Again about forty years ago, economists developed a theory of education, emphasizing its monetary costs and benefits. Economists have elaborated on these costs and benefits, including such possibilities as incorrect information about the benefits of education, the effect of peer groups on learning, and students' impatience. Identity economics puts more meat on these old bones. The lion's share of the costs of staying in school, and also of working hard at it, come from norms. How much schooling students get—what is called "the demand for education"—is largely determined by who they think they are and whether they should be in school. Good schools— schools with low dropout rates and high academic achievement —transform students' identities and norms. We thus address the two fundamental questions in the economics of education: who is enrolled in school and why, and what makes schools succeed or fail.

The final part of the book looks ahead. We discuss how identity economics makes use of new evidence and why economists, like scientists, should be receptive to data from close observation. We also discuss how identity expands economic inquiry. For example, identity widens the scope of choices that economists should study. People often have some choice over their identity. Parents choose schools for their children. Women may choose to pursue a career or stay at home. Immigrants choose whether to assimilate. Men and women choose whether to be single or to marry. In this way, people's motives, or tastes, are partly of their own making. Choice of identity, then, may be the most important "economic" decision a person ever makes. Second, identity points us to a new reason why preferences can change. Third parties may have incentives to change who people think they are, as well as their norms. Advertisers, politicians, and employers all manipulate social categories and norms. Finally, identity gives us a new window on inequality. Norms can call for behavior that leads to underperformance and unemployment. Boundaries of race, ethnicity, and class also limit who people can be. Because identity is fundamental to behavior, such limits may be the most important determinant of economic position and well-being.

THREE

Identity and Norms in Utility

WE NOW COME TO THE foundation of the book. This chapter shows precisely how we bring identity into economic analysis. All economic studies begin with a description of people's motivations. Here we build a new, augmented, utility function, which includes identity, norms, and categories.

The Basic Procedure

Our utility function is simple and parsimonious. With just three ingredients—categories, norms and ideals, and identity utility—we capture how motivations vary with social context. Our procedure has two parts. In Part 1 we specify the standard components of utility: a person's tastes for goods, services, or other economic outcomes. In Part 2 we specify the identity elements for the relevant social context:

• The *social categories* and each individual's category assignment, or *identity*.

- The *norms* and *ideals* for each category.
- The *identity utility*, which is the gain when actions conform to norms and ideals, and the loss insofar as they do not.

The last ingredient contains possible *externalities*. Economists say an externality occurs when one person's action hurts or benefits another person. A classic example of a negative externality is air pollution from a factory. In the case of identity, people's utility may increase or decrease, not only because of their own choices but also from the choices of others. Just as people suffer from a factory's pollution, they may suffer a loss if others violate norms. And just as people protest pollution, the injured party may protest or punish violations of the norms. We will see such losses in identity utility and concomitant responses in several studies in this book.

With this procedure, how do we, as analysts, specify the relevant social categories and norms? We base them on observation, as we will see in all the applications in this book.

This procedure gives us an enhanced utility function, with new trade-offs. An action may increase consumption but decrease identity utility. Just as in all economic analysis, we suppose that a person "maximizes utility" by balancing these trade-offs. And just as in all economic analysis, the notion of "maximizing utility" should not be taken to imply conscious choices on the part of an individual: it is a metaphor, and economists have an expansive interpretation of its meaning. (We discuss this and other tacit meanings of economists' vocabulary in the "Rosetta Stone" postscript at the end of this chapter.)

Short-Run and Long-Run Choices

In the simplest case, we suppose a person chooses actions to maximize her utility, given her identity, the norms, and the social categories. She balances her Part 1 standard utility and her Part 2 identity utility. The analysis is similar to studying supply and demand in the short run, where consumers and firms make decisions, given a fixed technology and a fixed market structure.

To some extent individuals may choose not only their actions but also their identity. Social categories are more or less ascriptive; but people often have some choice over who they are. As we noted before, for example, immigrants can decide whether to assimilate. Studying these decisions would be a long-run analysis, similar again to supply and demand, where, in the long run, firms and consumers can exit or enter a market. This choice of identity, again, is not necessarily conscious.

In the long run, also, people can change norms and ideals and the very nature of the social categories. These changes can be influenced by interested third parties, such as firms and politicians. Once again, this process is similar to that of supply and demand where, in the long run, technology evolves as a result of forces both within and outside the market.

Example: Smoking

Smoking trends in the United States offer a simple example. Smoking is a significant economic and social problem. The Centers for Disease Control and Prevention lists smoking as the leading preventable cause of death in the United States.[1] Productivity losses due to smoking have been estimated at $82 billion per year.[2] Economists have long studied cigarette use, as in the National Bureau of Economic Research's (NBER) substance use program, which also researches the use of alcohol and illegal drugs.

The typical economic study focuses on the demand for cigarettes. Demand comes from a utility function with tastes for smoking: some people simply enjoy it. More elaborate analyses take account of the addictive nature of nicotine and the enjoyment of smoking with friends. Central questions include how cigarette taxes affect cigarette consumption, particularly among teenagers.

To build an identity economics theory of smoking, we would begin the same way. We would first specify the standard utility for tobacco and nicotine. We would then specify the identity ingredients, relying on observation.

The norms for smoking have changed dramatically over the twentieth century, particularly for women. Early in the century, it was not respectable for women to smoke. In the 1960s, smoking was still more acceptable for men than for women.[3] The difference in attitudes ended with the Women's Movement in the 1970s. Beyond the scholarly research, consider the Virginia Slims advertising campaign and its slogan "You've Come a Long Way, Baby."[4] Women's lib, as pictured in the ads, freed women from laundry tubs, frumpy dresses, and the prohibition against smoking.[5] Following our procedure, we posit the social categories as men and women; the norms for men and women according to the era; and the losses in utility from deviating from the norm.

The utility function quite obviously predicts that the differences in smoking between men and women would initially be large but would converge after the 1970s. In the 1920s, almost 60 percent more men than women smoked.[6] In 1950, it was still less common for women to smoke than men.[7] By 1990, the gap was all but closed.[8] This convergence cannot be explained by standard economic theory, which would tell us to look for changes in economic differences between men and women (such as the decline in the gap between men's and women's earnings). But such explanations are inadequate, since even women with high incomes did not smoke in the initial period.

Smoking gives a clear example of the role of social norms. The change in gender norms was the single most important reason for the increase in women's smoking in the United States. Current economic theory suggests high taxes as a way to discourage smoking. But high taxes are both difficult to impose and difficult to enforce. Identity economics widens the search both for the causes and the cures.

A Rosetta Stone

BECAUSE THE GOAL of this book is to bring a new concept into economics, we must use the language of economics, which has many tacit conventions and metaphors. The language of economics is quite expansive; it should not be taken too literally. This postscript explains our use of various terms that take on meanings and connotations in economics that are different from common parlance and usage in other social sciences. (We provide these explanations for interested readers; others may want to skip to the next chapter.)

Individual Choice and Maximizing a Utility Function

In our analysis—as in almost all contemporary economics—people's decisions are described as maximizing their individual utility functions. That description may seem to imply that the choices are conscious. Conscious choice is only one possibility, and economists have a more expansive view. Utility maximization can also describe choices that people take unconsciously. Amartya Sen notes that physicists use the same technique when they say that light "follows the principle of least time." Of course, light does not make a conscious decision. But from the perspective of the human observer, it behaves as if it does.[1] Milton Friedman, who among economists was at the opposite end of the political and ideological spectrum from Sen, similarly held that utility maximization makes no presumption about the level of individual consciousness.[2]

The Role of Socialization

Such agnosticism regarding individual consciousness in utility maximization and in our formulation of identity then bridges some of the gap between economic analysis and the other social sciences. In many fields of social science, researchers see individuals' behavior as largely due to socialization rather than to conscious agency. People act as they do, naturally and without question, mostly out of habit. They are products of their social environment and unaware that they might have behaved quite differently. At the merry-go-round, for example, the waving four-year-olds have no conception that they could have behaved like the surly thirteen-year-old. It is only the social scientist observer who conceives of such a possibility. A standard economic model, on the other hand, takes no account of socialization, unless everyone is socialized in the same way. Any differences between people are seen as idiosyncratic personal differences.

Our identity model allows for both possibilities. People have individualistic tastes in their utility functions, but norms also enter into it. Individuals acquire some of these tastes and learn some of these norms as members of their communities. These norms may be internalized through mechanisms of community approval and disapproval. Gossip, stories, and private and public censure are common ways of communicating and reinforcing norms.

Individuals' decisions, then, in our framework, are driven not only by idiosyncratic tastes but also by internalized social norms.

The procedure of this chapter regarding how to specify a utility function thus allows a synthesis.

The Relation between Welfare and Utility

It is common for economists to relate the maximization of utility to the maximization of welfare. But in this book we never use the utility function in this way. To us, here, the utility function is simply a description of motivation.

Structure and "Choice of Identity"

In our analysis, we sometimes describe people as choosing their identity. Again, this phrasing could imply conscious choice, but we make no such presumption. People may just try and fit in; they may simply feel more or less comfortable in different situations. Some, such as the journalist Jill Nelson, whose autobiography we quote below, can articulate the trade-offs they make, but others would be unable to describe their motives and might not be even fully aware of them.

Moreover, in many cases, people have limited choice over identity. In any economic analysis, a choice is always paired with a description of the limitations on that choice. Here, social structures can limit choice. In a society where social categories are defined by race, family background, and ethnicity, for example, it may be virtually impossible for an individual to adopt a new identity. Our framework takes account of such situations.

Models and Defining Identity

Over the past century, increasingly, economists have built "models" to describe economic and social phenomena. Useful models, like revealing cartoons, focus on interesting features of the situation. Our procedure describes a new "part" that can be put into our models. Our focus, what we mean by identity, is well defined in the context of all models where we use the concept. There is no reason to dispute that meaning.

This methodology then avoids semantic debates, such as "What do we mean by identity?" If someone else should make another model and define identity differently, we should be equally willing to entertain her definition. The real debate is deferred to a different stage and can only be resolved empirically: does the model, with the new identity part, reach new and revealing conclusions?

Defining Should

We often say that people have notions—norms—of how they and others *should* behave. *Should* could imply ethical or moral views. However, we apply a more expansive meaning of *should*. How people *should* behave can refer to a social code, which can be largely internalized and even largely unconscious. For example, we dress up to deliver a formal lecture; we *should not* deliver it wearing shorts and sandals. There is no moral reason for dressing up, but shorts and sandals would be inappropriate, except maybe on a campus in southern California.

The world is full of such social codes, much more powerful in effect and affect. And much of the observance of such norms is unconscious. In this sense, our use of the word *norms* corresponds to much of the usage outside economics.

Individualistic Identity versus Interactionist Identity

We talk of an individual maximizing a utility function that specifies the social norms and the individual's preferences, or tastes. This description, on its face, describes what might be called an individualistic view of identity. An individual—in the absence of others—enjoys a gain in "identity utility" when she adheres to the norms for her category. But again, we have a more expansive view. This gain in identity utility can represent the enjoyment people experience when they do something that makes them fit in with a group. It also can represent the gains from differentiating one group from another. The utility then derives from group processes.

This wider view of our identity utility matches an interactionist understanding of identity among sociologists and anthropologists, where identities and norms emerge from social interactions and power relations. People in different groups or classes adopt common signs to differentiate themselves from those in other groups or classes.[3] Our analysis, moreover, can capture the dynamics between individuals and groups and show how one particular activity can emerge as a group's defining norm. Such an outcome occurs in our study of race and poverty.

FOUR

Where We Fit into Today's Economics

IDENTITY ECONOMICS IS AT the frontier. We follow the trajectory of the past fifty years and bring economics closer to reality. We change economics by closely observing economic and social life and transforming existing theory.

Consider four previous transformations. Fifty years ago, economic theory mostly considered two market structures: perfect competition and monopoly. But many industries—including the automobile, airline, and oil industries—do not fit either mold. To study such major parts of economies, economists adapted game theory. This entails the specification of who the actors are, what they know, the timing of their decisions, and their choice of strategies—all from observation of the specific context. Game-theoretic studies now pervade economics, covering topics from marriage to monetary policy.

Fifty years ago, too, economic studies assumed all participants in a market had the same information as everyone else. Nothing was hidden from the buyer or the seller. But now, in studying product markets, insurance markets, and labor contracts, we understand that information is asymmetric. We specify who knows what and when they know it.

More recently, behavioral economics has made theory more consistent with the findings of psychology. Now economists commonly talk of deviations from perfect rationality, such as present bias, habit formation, and loss aversion.

Finally, following Gary Becker, economists also study social problems. Discrimination, dysfunctional families, and crime have called for a new approach. Becker's approach, like ours, was to expand the utility function.

This book thus follows a long tradition of progress in economics. As in each of these four transformations, we seek to bring theory closer to observation. Our work emphasizes the individual in the social setting.

Experiments and Identity Economics

As in behavioral economics, a large body of experimental research informs our theory. Experiments in social psychology, and now increasingly in economics, show that individuals' behavior depends on who people think they are.

In 1954, in a foundational experiment, the psychologist Muzafer Sherif and his colleagues took two groups of eleven-year-old boys from Oklahoma City to Robbers Cave State Park.[1] The groups were sent on separate buses and were isolated in different parts of the park for a week. Within each group, the boys became close, mainly through roughing it together away from home. The boys formed distinct identities: one group killed a rattlesnake and proudly named themselves the Rattlers. The other group called themselves the Eagles. By the end of the week, both the Rattlers and the Eagles were aware that the other group was also inhabiting the park; but they had not yet met. Then they were brought together to play competitive games. The eleven-year-old equivalent of war broke out. At its climax, the two groups raided each other's huts and burned each other's flags. In the second phase of the experiment, researchers studied and applied interventions that would lead the boys to become friends. They happily returned home.

This experiment clearly exhibits the elements of our procedure: social categories (the groups identified themselves as Eagles and Rattlers); norms (both groups saw fighting as appropriate to the situation); and identity utility (the boys derived pride from their experiences).

Whereas the Robbers Cave experiment induced this behavior by bringing boys to a snake-infested forest, subsequent experiments by the psychologist Henri Tajfel and his colleagues sought minimal conditions that would create such group identification. These experiments took place in a university lab. This time the subjects were fourteen- and fifteen-year-old boys in Bristol, England. They were told that they had been divided into two groups according to whether they liked paintings by Paul Klee and Wassily Kandinsky. In fact, the assignments were random. When asked to choose from a list, subjects were more likely to choose the pair of points that maximized the relative difference in points between the groups, rather than the pair which gave their group the highest absolute number of points.[2]

Social psychologists have now applied this "minimal group paradigm" to almost every possible domain. For example, Alexander Haslam has reported on its relevance to leadership, conflict management, and group productivity in organizations.[3]

In a recent development, the economists Yan Chen and Sherry Li adopt this paradigm and show that group divisions matter even when there are monetary stakes.[4] Subjects were assigned into two groups (in one treatment, by preference for Klee and Kandinsky paintings; in another treatment, at random), and this time they were given tokens that could be redeemed for real money. When put in pairs to play strategic games, subjects could also, at a cost to themselves, "punish" or "reward" the other player. In their play, they exhibited in-group preferences: they gave more to in-group members, rewarded in-group members more, and punished out-group members more.[5]

Some economic experiments have further embellished this paradigm to create particular relations between groups in the lab. Kendra McLeish and Robert Oxoby at the University of Calgary used a particularly clever design to make people think that those in the other group were not as smart as themselves. In later play, the researchers observed a strong in-group bias.[6] Other experimenters have divided subjects into groups and induced "status" differences by giving members of one group gold-star stickers or giving one group a nice meal. These manipulations also led to biases in later play.[7]

Another type of experiment from social psychology also shows that social categories significantly affect behavior. People behave differently when they are reminded, even subtly, of their racial, ethnic, and gender identities. The method is called "priming." Claude Steele and Joshua Aronson conducted a classic experiment with Stanford undergraduates.[8] They gave African-American and white students hard questions from the verbal Graduate Record Examination. Some subjects were told in advance that the test would be diagnostic of their abilities; a control group received no such message. The African-American students who had received the message performed significantly worse than whites and African-American controls. Steele and Aronson argue that the students were affected by stereotypes of race-related performance and that the underperformance was due to what they have termed "stereotype threat."

These results are truly remarkable, especially given the subject pool and the context. To be admitted to Stanford, the subjects must have performed well on the Scholastic Aptitude Test, which is the sort of test Steele and Aronson administered. As Stanford students, if not before, they must also have lived in a mixed-race environment. Nor does the priming message or experiment seem like much of a threat. After all, the test had no consequence. Yet stereotype threat is a robust finding that has been now identified among many subject groups and stereotypes—including women and mathematics, and the elderly and memory.[9]

We are particularly struck by the recent experiments of the economists Karla Hoff and Priyanka Pandey investigating stereotype threat and caste in India. Subjects were asked to solve mazes and were paid a substantial amount of money for each maze they completed. In India, surnames reveal caste. When caste was primed by taking a roll call by last name, the low-caste subjects solved 23 percent fewer mazes.[10] Just hearing last names read aloud publicly was enough to lower performance, despite the significant monetary incentive for success.[11]

Identity-related experiments in economics like those of Chen and Li, and Hoff and Pandey, differ from traditional experiments in social psychology in that real monetary stakes are involved. They also differ from traditional economic experiments in that subjects are put in different social situations. The usual economic experiment tests an economic theory, such as the effect of some monetary incentive. To do so, the experimenter has to strip away social context. Subjects are anonymous: they do not see or know others with whom they are interacting. In contrast, identity-related experiments control for economic incentives and vary the social context. To study real-life social divisions, experimenters prime subjects or identify who is interacting with whom. They also create social divisions in the laboratory—as in the minimal-group experiments.

A growing number of economics experiments using classic games—like the "trust game," "dictator game," and "public goods game"—also find effects of real-world social divisions. The trust game, for example, is reminiscent of bank loans. Subjects are paired. The "sender" chooses how much money to give to the "receiver." The experimenter then triples this amount. The "receiver" then decides how much to give back to the "sender." In an experiment at Harvard, subjects sent back significantly less money when their partner was of a different race or nationality.[12] In Israel, Chaim Fershtman and Uri Gneezy's subjects sent back less money to Eastern Jews than to Ashkenazi Jews.[13] And Lorenz Goette, David Huffman, and Stephan Meier used the prisoner's dilemma game with Swiss Army platoons. For a price, subjects could punish those who did not cooperate. Subjects punished members from their own platoon more.[14] Experiments also find gender effects: in public-good games and in competitive settings, men and women subjects act differently when placed in groups with only women, only men, or mixed groups.[15]

All these experiments offer empirical support for identity economics. They all involve social categories, individuals in those categories, and norms for how group members should behave and interact with others. Different experimental contexts—which induce different identity utilities—then lead to different outcomes.

Identity Economics, Gary Becker, and Tastes

For years now, economists have augmented standard economics to take into account all sorts of different motivations observed in real life. The modern approach to this broadening of economics began in 1957 with Gary Becker's pathbreaking book *The Economics of Discrimination*.[16] As he writes in the introduction to the second edition, the University of Chicago Press originally objected to publishing the book in its Economic Research Studies series because discrimination was outside the domain of economics.[17] While sociologists and anthropologists studied the social causes and consequences of discrimination by whites against blacks, Becker studied the market implications. To do so, he built a new utility function, with a "taste for discrimination": "If an individual has a 'taste for discrimination,'" Becker writes, "he must act *as if* he were willing to pay something directly or in the form of reduced income, to be associated with some persons instead of others."[18] Becker then went on to study the effects on labor markets of such preferences.[19] Among the best-known theoretical conclusions is that a competitive marketplace would eliminate the effects of discrimination, since firms that discriminate to indulge these tastes will be replaced by firms that simply hire the most efficient workers. Becker continued with theories of fertility, crime and punishment, marriage, altruism, and addiction, among other things.[20] In each case he changed the utility function and showed how economics can be applied to study the forces that shape behavior. The costs and benefits of having children, for example, will affect fertility rates, and a marriage tax will affect marriage rates.

Many economists have followed Becker down this path of inquiry, and Becker himself continues to select noneconomic motivations to include in utility functions. But, by and large, these tastes are not assumed to vary with social context. Basic tastes are assumed to be universal, and any variation is attributed to idio-syncratic differences and personal experiences. And even when tastes derive from one's cultural background (as in the taste for pork), they are ultimately regarded as garden-variety prefer-ences such as that for oranges over bananas.[21] The research then focuses on how prices and income, not tastes, affect be-havior.[22] This approach, of course, corresponds to traditional economics experiments, which focus on monetary incentives, and differs from the new experiments, which show how social context matters.

Becker's basic observations—for example, that people like having children or that people enjoy smoking more when they smoke with friends—are perhaps more self-evident than those which motivate this book. But all it takes to observe norms is knowing how and where to look. Anthropologists, psychologists, and sociologists focus particularly on the relation between people's norms and their view of self and social context, largely because these researchers are sensitized by their theoretical ori-entation. Erving Goffman (of merry-go-round fame) titled one of his best-known books *The Presentation of Self in Everyday Life*.[23] Such presentations of self are just the sort of everyday clue we follow.

Norms in Economics

In identity economics, we presume that people follow norms much of the time because they want to do so. They internalize the norms and adhere to them. This conception does not cor-respond to economists' usual view. To date, economists have mostly seen norms as sustained by external forces: people follow a norm because if they do not, they could be punished in some way.

Consider an honor code, such as the Cadet Code of Honor of the U.S. Military Academy at West Point: it stipulates that "a cadet will not lie, cheat, steal, or tolerate those who do."[24] Not only is cheating a violation of the honor code, but failing to report violations of the code is also itself a violation. By induction, failing to report failures to report violations are also violations of the code. And all violations of the code, whether by commission or omission, are to be punished. When this string works, no one will cheat, and the honor code will be obeyed, even if no one believes in it.[25] The honor code is then a norm in the usual economic definition.

The honor code at West Point does work quite well most of the time, and the cadets are indeed afraid of severe punishment (usually expulsion) for violations. But the code would also break down if no students believed in it at all. Why? Because the long string of reports and failures to report cannot be sustained. Students would be able to dredge up some good excuse for failing to report an infraction by someone else. And punishments for not reporting of not reporting etc., would be increasingly difficult to justify. In the end, if no one at all believed in the honor code, it would break down.

The standard economics view of the honor system is just one example of norms arising out of ongoing interactions and threats of future punishments. In such "repeated games," actors' current violations can lead to losses in the future.[26] Michihiro Kandori, for example, has a theory of norms within a community: if one person cheats, a contagion of cheating ensues. This contagion eventually leads to systemic breakdown, and the ensuing loss to community members ultimately outweighs the initial gain from cheating.[27] In "coordination games," actors are concerned with making a choice that will help them coordinate well with others they meet in the future (like choosing to learn a foreign language or choosing a software program). The action chosen by most people then determines the norm. Peyton Young shows how norms emerge when actors encounter both people in their own communities and outsiders.[28]

Even absent such ongoing interactions, following a norm is also seen as a way to prove something important about yourself to others. In Douglas Bernheim's theory of conformity, for example, following a norm is construed as a type of signal.[29] David

Austen-Smith and Roland Fryer use a signaling model to try to understand why black students seem to have a norm of not working hard in school.[30] They posit that the students want to signal to their peers that they are the type of person who will remain in the neighborhood and can be counted on.

We include desire to follow norms in the utility function because a large amount of evidence indicates that those who follow norms do so because they believe in them.[31] The students at West Point really do believe in their honor code. Fear of punishment, wanting to coordinate with others, and wanting to appear reliable are all valid and important reasons for following norms. But even in a small, tight-knit community, at least some level of belief in the norms for their own sake is necessary to prevent norms from unraveling. Thus, norms may be what the political scientist Jon Elster calls the "cement of society."[32] We see the same theme in Elinor Ostrom's impressive body of work, conducted over decades—studying irrigation ditches, woodlands, and fisheries. The tragedy of the commons did not occur, because norms held the communal systems together.[33]

Where Do Norms Come From?

A growing number of researchers are now exploring the origins and economics of norms and identity. How do social norms change and evolve? How are they internalized? In Robert Oxoby's theory, people need norms to adapt psychologically to disadvantageous environments.[34] Roland Bénabou and Jean Tirole provide insight into the cognitive aspects of norms: people may invest in certain understandings of themselves and wish to preserve these images for themselves and others.[35] Work by Ulrich Horst, Alan Kirman, and Miriam Teschl suggests that norms may evolve to maintain a sense of belonging.[36] Most recently, Robert Akerlof has suggested a new and different approach. He argues that people desire confirmation of their beliefs. When actors with such utility functions interact, groups, norms, and identities emerge.[37]

35

Summary

In this first part of the book we have presented our procedure for bringing identity into economic analysis and discussed how including identity is both a continuation of past economics and a departure from it. We now study four areas where identity economics yields new conclusions.

Part Two

Work and School

FIVE

Identity and the Economics
of Organizations

R-DAY IS THE FIRST day at the United States Military Academy at West Point. The new cadets strip to their underwear. Their hair is cut off. They are put in uniform. They then must address an older cadet with the proper salute and the statement: "Sir, New Cadet Doe reports to the cadet in the Red Sash for the first time as ordered." New cadets must stand and salute, and repeat—again and again and again—until they get it exactly right, while being reprimanded for even the smallest mistake.

What could the Army be trying to accomplish? Perhaps the new cadets are learning skills they will need in their new jobs. But why the haircut? Why the red sash? Why the uniform? Why the ritual? David Lipsky, who tracked a company of cadets for their four years at West Point, says: "On R-Day you surrender your old self in stages."[1] It is only the beginning of the personal reengineering to come. West Point's mission is to produce leaders "committed to the values of Duty, Honor, Country" and "prepared for a career of professional excellence and service to the Nation."[2] The cadets will learn to march in step, to obey orders, and to lead in battle. They will come to think of themselves as officers in the U.S. Army.

Economists' current picture of organizations and work incentives cannot account for R-Day. Current economic theories do not capture duty and honor. They cannot explain how the recruits, or workers, regard how they *should* behave. Nor is there a place for an organization that would want to change those views. In this chapter, we build such missing motivations into the economics of organizations and work.

Much current economics deals with a basic problem facing business owners: how to give workers appropriate incentives. A worker's individual performance can be hard to observe. On a factory floor, it is hard to see how tightly a worker turns a screw or how neatly he packs a box. In retail sales, it is hard to see how much effort a salesperson exerts when trying to sell a product to a customer. How is the owner of the factory or retail establishment to compensate the worker? How much should she pay him, and according to what criteria? Economic theory suggests that, although the owner cannot perfectly observe what a worker does, she usually can make some observations that might be useful. At the factory, she might test the products at random and record the failure rate of the product. In retail sales, she might observe sales receipts at the end of each day. A worker could then be paid more when the failure rate is low, and a sales clerk could be paid more when sales are high. The theory then gives us a neat solution to this problem. A worker should be given incentives by this high and low pay, and also paid just enough on average to take on the risk.

While economic theory suggests these neat answers, it also strongly suggests why such monetary incentives will not work well in practice.[3] First, output is often produced by teams of workers, rather than individuals. As a result, the information that is the potential basis for compensation—such as the product failure rate or the end-of-day sales receipts—is only weakly related to the effort of the individual worker. Many people are ultimately responsible for success, and without direct observation of effort, it is impossible to give individual workers their due.[4]

Second, many jobs involve multiple tasks. If a worker's rewards are based on only some of her tasks, that is where she will concentrate her effort. For example, a CEO whose compensation depends on the current stock price will try to run up the current stock price but will ignore the long-term consequences.

Third, sometimes rewards are based on relative performance, as when workers compete for a promotion. Such tournaments reduce management's need for information because workers are compensated only for relative performance. But tournaments create another problem: workers have an incentive to sabotage one another.[5]

Empirical research confirms the problems of team production, multitasking, and tournaments: people respond too well to monetary incentives. Brian Jacob and Steven Levitt have shown the depth of the problem.[6] When principals and teachers are evaluated on the basis of their students' test scores, it is commonly believed that teachers "teach to the test." Jacob and Levitt found that some Chicago teachers found an easier way to raise scores: they just changed their students' answer sheets. Robert Gibbons of MIT has concluded that "firms get what they pay for." But because pay cannot be well targeted, firms often do not get what they actually want.[7] All this research indicates that if an organization is going to function well, it should not rely solely on monetary incentives.

We argue that identity is central to what makes organizations work. Workers should be placed in jobs with which they identify, and firms should foster such attachments.[8] We are not alone. Timothy Besley and Maitreesh Ghatak of the London School of Economics and Canice Prendergast of the University of Chicago have argued similarly that production is enhanced when an organization hires workers who share its mission.[9] Such organizations work well because an employee who identifies with the firm needs little monetary inducement to perform her job well.[10]

An Identity Model of Work Incentives

Here we follow the procedure outlined in Chapter 3 to incorporate identity into the economics of organizations and work

incentives.[11] We start with Part 1 and specify the standard economics of organizations. We use what we call a "boilerplate
model" that captures this economics in the most elementary
form. Such a stripped-down model is standard fare for first-year
economics graduate students. It highlights the problem, discussed above, of determining appropriate incentives when individual worker effort is hard to see. We then move to Part 2
and add the identity ingredients: (1) social categories, (2) norms
and ideals, and (3) losses and gains in identity utility. These factors considerably change how the firm will pay its workers and
how it will treat them.

The Procedure: Part 1. In the boilerplate model, there is a firm
owner, who is called the *principal,* and a worker, who is called the
agent. The agent chooses to exert either high or low effort. High
effort increases the likelihood that the firm's revenues will be
high. The principal cannot observe the agent's effort, but she
can observe whether revenues are high or low. The principal
can influence the worker's effort by paying more if revenues are
high than if they are low. The standard economics problem is to
derive this pay: the wage the principal will pay the agent when
revenue is high and the wage when revenue is low.

The Procedure: Part 2. How will considerations of identity
change the incentive scheme? Drawing from observation of
many workplaces, we add our three identity ingredients.

Social Categories. We classify workers into two types. Those who
identify with their firm (or organization) we call *insiders.* Those
who lack such identification—those who do not identify with
the firm—we call *outsiders. Insiders* and *outsiders* are then the social categories for our model.

Norms and Ideals. We suppose that an insider thinks she *should*
work on behalf of the firm. Her ideal is to exert high effort. In
contrast, an outsider thinks she should put in minimum effort—
she thinks only about herself, not about the organization she
works for.

Gains and Losses in Identity Utility. Very simply, we suppose that
an insider loses identity utility when she puts in low effort rather
than high effort. An outsider, on the other hand, loses identity

utility when she puts in high effort for an organization of which she feels no part.

How do these identity ingredients change the nature of the contract that induces the worker to put in high effort? If the worker is an insider, identity utility will reduce the bonus needed to induce high effort. That is, there will be less difference between the high-revenue wage and the low-revenue wage.[12] The explanation is straightforward: an insider maximizes her identity utility by exerting high effort. She does not need a large additional difference in monetary reward to induce her to work hard.[13] In contrast, an outsider loses identity utility from working hard. A higher wage differential is needed to induce her to work hard to compensate her for this loss in identity utility.

Would a firm be willing to invest in a worker to make him an insider rather than an outsider? The answer is yes. An insider is willing to work harder for lower overall pay. When the pay difference is great enough, it is worthwhile for the firm to invest in changing workers' identities.

But changing a worker's identity can be costly, involving expenditures on training, sign-on bonuses, and benefits. The model tells us when a firm's overall profits are likely to increase from investment in worker identity. Profits increase and a firm will undertake this investment if: (1) inculcating identity is cheap, (2) there is much underlying economic uncertainty, (3) workers' effort is hard to observe, (4) revenues or output depend on special exertion at peak times, (5) workers especially dislike risk, and (6) high effort is critical to the organization's output.

The Model and Military-Civilian Differences

Let's consider the model's implications for military-civilian differences. It is relatively cheap to impart identity to soldiers and officers in the U.S. armed forces because, as volunteers, they tend to be inherently sympathetic to its goals. In addition, military personnel are especially susceptible to indoctrination because of their relative isolation from civilian life. It is also often very costly to quit (for example, Lipsky reports that for many cadets, West Point is the only affordable college education). In the military there is often little relation between outcome and individual effort—especially in battle.[14] Hence, the model predicts that the military will rely on identity rather than on monetary compensation.[15]

This prediction is consistent with the weak dependence of pay on performance in the military. Historically, promotions in the U.S. Army and Navy were either "up" or "out," and rank and pay were based almost solely on seniority.[16] Even today, pay differentials between high- and low-ranking officers are much smaller than corresponding pay differences in the corporate world.[17] And in the military, when outstanding individual effort is observed, medals—not bonuses—are awarded.[18]

Motivation for the Model

We based our model on the findings of the considerable literature outside of economics on the military and civilian workplace. A distillation of this work shows the match between the *insider-outsider* model and the motivation of both military personnel and civilian workers.

The Military

Many different sources, including officer guides, autobiographies, sociological studies, and military history, show a close match with our model. In the model there is a division between insiders and outsiders. Insiders have an *ideal* of how they should or should not behave, and they lose utility if they fail to live up to that ideal. The reactions to others' behavior were left out, but they could easily have been included as well. The model mirrors the real military whose members emphasize the distinction between military (insiders) and civilians (outsiders). Military academies and training programs purposefully inculcate this distinction. They also instill the military code of conduct, which prescribes the norms for how an insider should behave. He should follow orders. The Air Force's ideal is "Service before

Self." In a properly functioning military organization, members, as insiders, adopt these ideals. The military relies on these ideals rather than on incentive pay.[19]

Every account we have read of military life emphasizes the distinction between military and civilian. For example, Omar Bradley, who was Dwight D. Eisenhower's next-in-command, wrote an autobiographical account of the Allied invasion of Europe. The title, *A Soldier's Story,* reveals both Bradley's identity and his ideals. Bradley reserved the term *soldier* for those deserving the highest praise, such as Generals George Patton, Harold Alexander, and Courtney Hodges. They too were *soldiers.* The leading military sociologists Charles Moskos, John Williams, and David Segal describe the nature of the ideal soldier: he should be "war oriented in mission, masculine in make-up and ethos, and sharply differentiated in structure and culture from civilian society."[20]

Official and semiofficial documents from all branches of the U.S. armed services further describe ideal behavior. For example, the *Air Force Guide* says that military service is a profession with "a sense of corporate identity." The officer must obey the rules of the organization and follow orders given in the chain of command. Moreover, he should not behave like an outsider, simply following those orders passively. Instead he should be an insider with "faith in the system." To "lose faith in the system is to place self before service."[21]

Military organizations actively promote such military identity. Ideals and prescriptions for behavior are clearly stated and taught in basic training and military academies. In terms of our model, the military makes investments to turn outsiders into insiders. Initiation rites, short haircuts, boot camp, uniforms, and oaths of office are among the obvious means of creating a common identity.[22] The routine of the military academies also shows some of the tools used to inculcate military identity. Harsh training exercises and hazing, like the R-Day rituals at West Point, are just one way the Army puts its imprint on cadets.[23] Of course, harsh training can also serve to impart specific knowledge and skills rapidly. But cognitive-dissonance theory from psychology suggests why such harsh training and hazing can also be effective at changing cadets' self-image. They must explain to themselves why they (seemingly willingly) accept such treatment. In formulating an answer, they adopt a new image of themselves.

The military's stress on "service before self" and its deemphasis of pecuniary rewards suggest—as in our model—that military identity can substitute for incentive pay. Thus, for example, General Ronald Fogleman of the Air Force reflects: "So what's the payoff for placing service before self? It isn't solely the paycheck or the benefits that keep us going. In my 32 years of service, I've met many men and women who embody this concept of service before self. They remain with the Air Force because of the intangibles—the satisfaction gained from doing something significant with their lives; the pride in being part of a unique organization that lives by high standards; and the sense of accomplishment gained from defending our nation and its democratic way of life."[24]

Ethnographies also record expressions of the ideal of service. For example, the sociologist Jeffrey McNally describes one West Point graduate, whom he calls Matt, who considered civilian employment after completing the five years of military service required after graduation. But Matt rejected civilian life, saying of the companies where he interviewed: "None of them ever really talked about what was important to me, and that was service. All they talked to me about was money."[25]

Military personnel are also turned from outsiders into insiders as a by-product of normal operations. Soldiers live and work in separation from civilians. They also have intense and extended interactions with each other, especially in combat units. Here we see that the nature of an organization itself—and how it divides personnel into workgroups—can affect identity and hence preferences and incentives. (We later describe workgroups in civilian companies.) During World War II, a team of sociologists studied the U.S. military, resulting in a large-scale study titled *The American Soldier*. They give this description of the ideal of a member of a combat unit: succinctly, he should be "a man." That meant "courage, endurance and toughness, . . . avoidance of display of weakness in general, reticence about emotional or idealistic matters, and sexual competency."[26] Although the authors observed that recruits initially behaved in this way to avoid ridicule, ultimately they internalized the ideal: "The fear of being thought less than a man by one's buddies can be as powerful a control factor as the fear of the guardhouse. [The] process . . . is internalized and automatized in the form of 'conscience.'"[27]

Finally, descriptions of discipline in the military allow another assay of identity and norms in economic models. The sociologist Kai Erikson emphasizes that disciplinary procedures reveal a community's boundaries and norms. Disciplinary proceedings not only punish offenders; they are also morality plays that define right and wrong.[28] In our language, they define the norms and ideals. The *Air Force Guide* is explicit about this role of discipline: "[The] constraint [of discipline] must be felt not so much in the fear of punishment as in the moral obligation that it places on the individual to heed the common interests of the group. Discipline establishes a state of mind that produces proper action and cooperation under all circumstances, regardless of obstacles."[29]

We see here a stark contrast with the characterization of discipline and punishment in standard economics. Discipline and punishment simply yield prices, to be paid upon breaking the rules. A person then breaks the rules if it is worth the price. At the celebration of his seventieth birthday, Gary Becker explained his original motivation for writing the paper "Crime and Punishment," which is perhaps the clearest statement of this idea.[30] Becker told of a day he was late for a student's oral exams. There were no legal places to park, so he parked illegally. He later decided that he needn't have felt guilty, since he was willing to pay the fine in exchange for arriving on time. Guilt and shame are thus absent from the economic theory of deviance.[31] Nor is there any economic theory where the role of discipline is to inculcate shame. For all punishments and rewards, the agent maximizes the same utility function. In contrast, discipline in the Air Force aims to alter airmen's "state of mind"; that is, to change their preferences.

Of course, severe punishments also play a direct role in the operation of a successful military. Lipsky's *Absolutely American* emphasizes cadets' internalization of West Point values, but an important subtext is the harsh penalties for those who do not meet the standards.[32] We view such punishments as controlling mavericks who do not adhere to the military ideal. A realistic extension to our model would include workers with little susceptibility to the identity program of the firm. Dismissal or other punishment would keep these workers under control.

The Civilian Workplace

Our model applies to the civilian as well as the military workplace. One of the central themes of the management literature is the dichotomy between "intrinsic" and "extrinsic" motivations. That distinction is also a major emphasis of our identity model, corresponding to the different motivations of insiders and outsiders. This dichotomy is also evident in the study of organizational behavior itself. Histories of this discipline invariably contrast the work of Frederick Taylor, with its origins in the early twentieth century, with the human relations movement that began with the study of the Hawthorne works of Western Electric in the 1930s. According to Taylor, management should define tasks, determine the best way to accomplish them, and pay for performance.[33] In terms of the model, Taylorism acts as if cooperation is automatic; it does not matter if workers are insiders or outsiders. But since the 1930s, management theory has emphasized the difficulties of monitoring workers' tasks and therefore the importance of individual or group-oriented motivations. In terms of the model, good management wants its workers to be motivated insiders, rather than to be alienated outsiders.

Current studies emphasize management's role in changing employee objectives. In terms of the model, effective management encourages workers to be insiders, who identify with the goals of the firm, rather than outsiders. Aligning the objectives of workers and management is the goal in the strategy called "management by objective," which gives employees a role in setting their own goals. Management by objective works largely by changing self-motivation. A manager of an accounting firm in a study by Mark Covaleski and coauthors summarized: "After a while [striving to exceed targeted objectives] had nothing to do with the bonuses. . . . It's the concept of having people fired up."[34] "Total quality management" (TQM) similarly aims to encourage workers to take pride in their work and thereby identify with their organization and its missions. The management consultants Thomas Peters and Robert Waterman have described how a company's commitment to customer service and to product quality ultimately pays off: employees are more motivated when they are proud of the company's products and services.[35] For example, Caterpillar promises to deliver parts for its vehicles and equipment within forty-eight hours anywhere on the globe. McDonald's instructs employees to throw away fries that are not piping hot. Policies that increase customer satisfaction, according to Peters and Waterman, also enhance workers' self-image and motivate them to accomplish the firm's goals.

Some of the most famous taskmasters in industry and commerce have been known for their enthusiasm for instilling company loyalty. Thomas Watson, the CEO of IBM, said: "Joining a company is an act that calls for absolute loyalty."[36] John Pepper, the successful CEO of Procter and Gamble, said: "We understand that we have joined not just a company, but an institution with a distinguished character and history that we are now responsible for perpetuating."[37] But such loyalty to an institution is apparent not just at the big and famous firms. Yale University's Truman Bewley conducted extensive interviews in Connecticut firms—mostly small—during the recession of the early 1990s. He found that the firms only rarely reduced wages, even though other workers could have been hired at lower pay. Bewley concluded that the firms kept pay high out of concern for workers' "capacity . . . to identify with their firm and to internalize its objectives."[38]

Down the Corporate Ladder

Ethnographies show that self-motivation and identification with the firm are important for workers at all levels. The role of identity in the day-to-day lives of wage earners is perhaps the most central finding of ethnographic work. Take the examples of Mike, as told by Studs Terkel, and Shirley, as told by the sociologist Vicki Smith.

Terkel's interview with Mike, a laborer in a Cicero, Illinois, steel mill, affirms the validity of the model, but in an unexpected place.[39] Mike is an outsider. He dislikes his job intensely and he feels insulted by his foreman. But he does not want to be unemployed either; so, for the most part, he shows only minor resistance while on the job. He does not "even try to think"; he refuses to say "Yes, sir" to his boss; and occasionally he "puts a little dent in [the steel] . . . to see if it will get by." Even so, his anger builds up, and after work he gets into tavern brawls. Why? "Because all day I wanted to tell my foreman to go fuck himself, but I can't." Mike's hostile behavior exactly fits the model. He is an outsider. He works rather than shirks, but only because of the monetary rewards. He loses identity utility because of the gap between the effort he expends and what he ideally would like to do. His off-the-job behavior, in our terminology, is his way to "restore his loss of identity utility." This example shows that even when pecuniary incentives are all that motivate a worker, identity does not lie dormant: its consequences are still visible. Furthermore, the anger Mike expresses and its consequences are predicted by identity economics, but they seem to have no place in current—including behavioral—economics.

Shirley, unlike Mike, is an insider. Shirley, an African American, works for a company Vicki Smith calls Reproco, a subcontractor for on-site clerical and mailroom workers. Recognizing the potential for conflict between its staff and the professionals in the companies it serves, Reproco trains its employees to deal with insults from clients. We see that despite daily insults, Shirley is a motivated worker who takes pride in her position. An exchange at a Philadelphia law firm with a white lawyer illustrates her attitude. When the lawyer expresses her impatience with the time needed to finish a photocopying job, Shirley responds politely, using her calculator to estimate the length of the queue. The lawyer walks off in a huff, telling Shirley,

"You are always just pushing those little buttons."[40] Shirley, however, maintains her composure. She explains to Vicki Smith, who is watching, that she is a "Reproco person." Calling on her work self enables her to keep calm. Had she instead expressed her anger (a low-effort response, according to the model), she would have lost identity utility for failing to live up to her ideal.

Every work ethnography we have read tells stories similar to those of Mike and Shirley: workers either identify with their jobs (like insiders in the model) or they are frustrated (like outsiders in the model, who put in high effort, but only to obtain the monetary incentives). Here are two more brief examples: Tom Juravich writes of a wire-factory worker whose in-your-face supervisor denies him permission to buy a new screwdriver to finish a job. In frustration, the worker hammers to pieces a spare part worth hundreds of dollars.[41] And Katherine Newman describes fast-food workers in Harlem and Washington Heights, New York, who, despite the grease, heat, customer disrespect, and low wages, still take pride in their uniforms.[42]

Is there any way to measure the extent to which workers identify with their organizations? The General Social Survey (GSS) is an annual national survey of demographic and attitudinal variables with a sample size of about three thousand people. It asks employees about job satisfaction, and the 1991 survey included a module about work organizations. According to our tabulations, 82 percent of employees disagreed, weakly or strongly, with the statement that they had little loyalty toward their work organization. 78 percent agreed that their values and those of their organization were similar. 90 percent were proud to be working for their organization. And 86 percent were very satisfied or moderately satisfied with their jobs. These fractions differed only marginally across gender and race, and between blue-collar versus white-collar occupations. Of course, these responses do not tell us why workers feel this way. Perhaps their firms invest in identity. Perhaps workers select organizations that share their values. Perhaps workers adopt their firms' values to minimize cognitive dissonance. All of these explanations fit our general framework. In each case, identity would be a component of workers' utility.

Identity Economics and Workgroups

Our discussion has assumed so far that insiders identify with their organizations and outsiders do not. This division, coarse as it may be, gives some insight into identity and the workplace. But many studies have found that workers typically identify with their immediate workgroup rather than with the organization as a whole. A finer model—with loyalty to a workgroup rather than loyalty to the firm as a whole—may be more realistic.

Small changes in our identity ingredients capture such workplace norms:

- *Social categories.* Workers identify themselves either as outsiders or as *members of a workgroup.*
- *Norms and ideals.* Workgroup members think that they should put in *medium* effort. In contrast, outsiders have an ideal of *low* effort.
- *Gains and losses in identity utility.* As before, workers lose identity utility insofar as their effort deviates from their respective ideals.

The degree to which employees identify with their workgroup or become outsiders depends on the company's management policy. On the one hand, the firm could have *strict supervision* of its workers: A supervisor would monitor workers closely and report on individual workers' efforts. Workers, however, would resent the close oversight and adopt outsider identities—like Mike. Later, we shall see such an outcome in the classic Bank Wiring Observation Room experiment. On the other hand, the firm could have *loose supervision,* where the supervisor would not report to upper management. In this case, the supervisor and the workers identify as workgroup members.

These two management styles have their respective advantages and disadvantages for the firm. Strict supervision yields more information regarding workers' efforts, enabling the principal to fine-tune monetary incentives. But because strict supervision converts workers into outsiders, their ideal is low effort.

Loose supervision provides less information on workers' effort, making monetary incentives harder to fine-tune. But workers' ideal is medium effort, not low effort. The latter—loose supervision with its workgroup identification and medium effort—is often the best management policy. The following examples compare this model to workplace realities.

Loose Supervision: A Machine Shop in Chicago

Twenty-five years apart, two University of Chicago PhD students in sociology, Donald Roy and Michael Burawoy, wrote participant-observer accounts of the same small-parts machine shop.[43] Both studies offer clear evidence of the way loyalty to the workgroup results in middle-level productivity associated with the norms of workgroup identification.

In this shop, a worker's pay was the higher of an hourly wage rate and a job-specific piece rate. Management aimed to set the piece rates so that it would be equally difficult in every job to reach the same monetary target. But they apparently did a bad job of it: many jobs were considered "gravy," tasks for which meeting the target—or "making out," in the language of the shop floor—was very easy. In Roy's time, there were also quite a few "stinkers," jobs for which the piece rate was so low that meeting the target was impossible. The workers hid all these discrepancies from management, and management also turned a blind eye to them.

In the model there is a workgroup norm, and workers lose utility insofar as they deviate from the ideal effort level. The employer may also find it profitable to let the workgroup norm of medium effort prevail. We see both in the machine shop. The norm, known to all employees in the shop, was to earn no more than 140 percent of base pay. They feared that higher output would trigger an investigation by the time-study men.[44] Moreover, norms of behavior were to make out and to aid others in doing so by evading the employer's rules. Such evasion involved beginning a new job before clocking out on the previous one (a strategy known as *chiseling*), avoiding production in excess of the output quota, and deceiving the time-study men.

Indeed, both Roy and Burawoy see the operators as having turned their work into a game where the goal was to make out. The pay from making out became the score in a game. Burawoy says that winning at this game was central to the self-concept of a machine operator:[45] "Making out," Burawoy writes, was a "form of self-expression," and also "an end in itself."[46] These feelings were shared by all the machine operators. "As Roy and I soon came to appreciate: if we were to be anyone in the shop, we had better begin making out."[47] Thus, while the workgroup norms subverted management's goal of fine-tuning job completion times, they did involve finishing a job in the time allocated (corresponding to the middle-level goals of a member of the workgroup in the model).

Roy's and Burawoy's accounts both raise the question: Why didn't the management run a tighter shop? The shop floor was crowded with auxiliary workers who were aware of the machinists' chiseling. Yet management failed to press these potential informants. Occasionally it sent time-study men onto the floor, but these management representatives allowed themselves to be hoodwinked by a variety of fairly obvious strategies. The model suggests an explanation for this lax oversight: the workers, operating according to their own norms, produced satisfactory results. Management feared that stricter supervision would turn the workers into outsiders and thus reduce productivity.

Strict Supervision: The Bank Wiring Observation Room

Another, earlier, sociological observation of workgroups, the Bank Wiring Observation Room experiment, shows what we could only guess from the Chicago machine shop: that workers' response to strict supervision may result in a decline in output. In 1931, the Western Electric Company, at the behest of the pioneering industrial sociologists Elton Mayo, F. J. Roethlisberger, and William Dickson, observed a small group of workers producing telephone switches in an isolated room in a communications equipment assembly plant.[48] As in the Chicago machine shop, the workers established a clear norm for effort: two switches per day. However, when a supervisor tried to take a hard line, instituting tough inspections, the workers retaliated. They sabotaged his work, and the two-switch norm fell apart. The company had to transfer the supervisor elsewhere.

Statistical Evidence: A Midwest Manufacturing Plant

Stanley Seashore's study of a heavy machinery plant in the Midwest gives statistical evidence suggestive of both the existence and the influence of workgroup norms. In this plant, workers were assigned to work units virtually at random.[49] From questionnaires, Seashore constructed an index of workgroup cohesion and analyzed its relation to individual worker productivity. If workgroup norms exist and affect productivity, we would expect individual productivity to vary more in noncohesive groups than in cohesive groups. This prediction is borne out in the data: variance in productivity was lower among individuals in cohesive groups. Also, because, theoretically, workgroups could have different norms, we would predict that variance between cohesive groups would be greater than that between noncohesive groups. Such a prediction was also borne out by the data.[50]

Lincoln Electric: Example or Counterexample?

The case of Lincoln Electric and its pay scheme, discussed by Paul Milgrom and John Roberts, has been widely cited as evidence in favor of the principal-agent theory.[51] It thus poses challenges to our conclusions. Base pay at Lincoln Electric was calculated on a piece-rate basis, and productivity was estimated to be three times that of comparable manufacturing plants, suggesting that financial incentives were effective in increasing worker effort and productivity. But a close look at Lincoln Electric suggests that management took special steps to avoid the usual problems with piece rates. Accounts of Lincoln emphasized its strong sense of community. Workers were quick to say that it was a special place. Management prided itself on being tough but fair and on showing unusual concern for workers. Furthermore, half of compensation came from a bonus based on management's subjective evaluation of each worker's overall performance, including cooperation.[52] Workers perceived these bonuses as fair, and management had accurate assessments. Our model suggests that management invested in creating unusually committed insider workers. According to the company president, James Lincoln, "there is no such thing in an industrial activity as Management and Men . . . being two different types of people."[53]

Workgroups in the Military

Loyalty to one's buddies is part and parcel of all accounts of military life. Thus it should come as no surprise that the military also shows us the importance of workgroup identity as well as the respective costs and benefits of loose and strict supervision. We saw earlier how combat units instill an ideal for behavior. In their memoir of the Vietnam War, Harold Moore and Joseph Galloway explain that they went to Vietnam because of a sense of duty to their country. But in battle, a tight bond developed among the soldiers, giving them the inspiration to fight: "We discovered in that depressing, hellish place, where death was our constant companion, that we loved each other. We killed for each other, we died for each other. . . . We held each other's lives in our hands."[54] Such feelings appear to be quite general within combat units. *The American Soldier* gives similarly poignant account of loyalty for buddies, as expressed by a soldier wounded in Sicily: "You would rather be killed than let the rest of them down."[55] This code of conduct is the ideal of the workgroup.

This loyalty has benefits for the organization because soldiers exert more than minimal effort; but, as in the workgroup model, it also has costs. In an interview on National Public Radio, General Theodore Stroup described the problems that arise from such loyalty to the unit.[56] When a member of their unit does something wrong, soldiers face a conflict: "When they get in a stress situation . . . [s]ubconsciously they may have their own internal argument that says, 'I know I must be loyal to my unit, but I must be loyal also to a higher authority, which is standard of conduct, rules of justice, rules of law.'" Stroup gave as an example the crew of the U.S. Navy submarine *Greeneville* that collided with a Japanese fishing trawler off the coast of Hawaii in 2001, killing nine people. The crew covered up for their skipper.[57]

The American Soldier provides statistical evidence of this dilemma: whether loyalty to the unit trumps loyalty to higher command.[58] In questionnaires, officers, privates, and noncommissioned officers were asked their opinion regarding appropriate discipline in different situations. The noncommissioned officers took a middle ground between the officers and the enlisted men. For example, interviewees were asked how they would behave "as a platoon sergeant [who] finds that one of the men in your barrack has brought a bottle of liquor into camp." Seventy percent of privates and 59 percent of noncommissioned officers, but only 35 percent of commissioned officers, said they would just "warn him to be careful and not do it again."[59]

Economics and Group Norms

This study of organizations sharply illustrates the difference between norms as we understand them and norms as explained by previous economic theories. As we have already discussed, economists have, of course, written about conformity to group norms. There is also an earlier answer to the question of why piece rates, which are the simplest incentive system, are so rare.[60] With piece rates, workers fear that if they complete jobs quickly, their firm will think the job is easy and will ratchet the piece rate downward. In the Chicago machine shop, as we have seen, workers solved this problem by establishing a norm that kept output at a certain level.

But what enforces adherence to the norm? In our model, as in the findings of Burawoy and Roy, it is part of a worker's identity. Workers feel that they should abide by this restriction; the norm is a goal in and of itself. In an extension of the model, workers would suffer utility losses if others disobeyed the norms, and would retaliate to prevent these losses. Any maverick will thus think twice about the consequences before violating the norms.

In contrast, the conventional explanation for the maintenance of such a norm is based on strategic behavior and ongoing interaction. As in the honor code at West Point, it is viewed as a repeated game: Why do the workers obey the norm in the first place? Because they believe that they will be punished if they do not. They feel that they will be punished because others fear punishment if they do not themselves punish, and so on, ad infinitum. In this outcome, everyone follows the group norm, but no one believes in it: they abide by it out of fear. But this reasoning simply does not reflect what we see and hear on the shop floor or in the trenches.

Shared Goals and Policy Conclusions

This chapter suggests that the success of an organization depends on employees who share its goals. Otherwise, the employees will game any pay scheme they are given. But our understanding of shared goals is more sophisticated and less literal than, for example, IBM employees sitting at their desks and obeying the corporate motto to "THINK." Rather, employees are assigned jobs, and they understand that it is their duty to do them. In our first model, they act alone, but in the extended, more realistic, formulation, they are acting as part of a workgroup. This is what it means for workers to identify with their organizations.

This interpretation is central to Max Weber's understanding of the modern firm. Weber perceived that in a bureaucracy, lower-level employees have information that is not necessarily available to those higher up. The principal-agent model captures this asymmetric information across levels. But missing is Weber's emphasis on *duty to office*. In his inimitable style: "An office is a vocation" and "entrance into an office . . . is considered an acceptance of a specific duty of fealty to the purpose of the office."[61] That, of course, is what it means to be an insider.

Clear policy conclusions follow from this identity economics view of the firm. One obvious implication concerns executive pay. We have already discussed how blunt monetary incentives can be. The more a CEO's compensation is based on stock options, for example, the greater is the incentive to maximize the price at which to cash in. There are at least two ways to do this: one is by increasing the firm's true value; another is by creatively managing the firm's books.[62] Recent evidence shows that executives have understood and embraced the second possibility. What can identity economics say about this state of affairs? In our model, and following Weber, the most important consideration in incentives for executives could be their role as *fiduciary*. Office holders should fulfill the duties of their office. If jobholders have only monetary rewards and only economic goals, they will game the system insofar as they can get away with it. But insofar as workers are insiders with the same goals as their organization, such conflict of interest disappears.

Another obvious lesson concerns management. Identity economics tells us that managers should do more than supervise workers' effort and determine the right incentive pay: they also play a critical role in making employees into insiders rather than outsiders. We see this possibility in workplace ethnographies of the successes and failures of management, as well as in the views of successful business leaders, such as John Whitehead and his fourteen principles at Goldman Sachs, and the management of Lincoln Electric who were with their "Men" on the shop floor.

Summary: Using Identity Economics and Drawing New Conclusions

This chapter provides our first extended application of identity economics. Using our model, we derive a basic new result: if employees think of themselves as firm insiders rather than outsiders, the pay differentials needed to induce high effort will be lower. The difficulties that arise when employees game incentive systems are also greatly reduced. Worker identification may therefore be a major factor, perhaps even the dominant factor, in the success or failure of organizations.

SIX

Identity and the Economics
of Education

FROM 1969 TO 1971, riots between white and black students at an upstate New York high school brought all classroom instruction to a halt.[1] The school was closed ten separate times in the academic year 1969–70. There was a drastic reduction in learning that no current economics can capture. There had been no change in the factors that economic theories would typically tell us to look for: no budget cuts, no reduction in the number or quality of teachers, no degradation of the school physical plant, and no change in the economic incentives for students to graduate.[2] Just as economists' understanding of work incentives and organization fails to explain the rituals at West Point, so the story of Hamilton High—like stories from many other schools—indicates that we need an identity economics theory of education.[3]

In this chapter we add identity to the economic theory of education. We consider students who want to fit in with their peers, and schools that are social institutions. The identity ingredients give a new window on what makes schools effective; why school-reform programs work or fail; and why students go to school, which is what economists call the "demand for education."

Current economic theories of education, for the most part, picture a student as a rational decision maker who weighs the economic costs and benefits of staying in school. Current theories, for the most part, also view a school as a factory. Textbooks, labs, the school building itself, the teachers, and the students' own talents and family background are its inputs. More or less productive workers are the "human capital" outputs. Such a view of students misses the fact that students care about their social position in school and how they fit in with their peers. Schools are not just mechanical factories that teach skills. Rather, as historians, sociologists, anthropologists, and educators explain, schools are institutions with social goals. Not only do they impart skills, but they also impart norms regarding who students should be and what they should become. These ideals affect how long students stay in school and also how much they learn while there.

In private, religious, and charter schools, these ideals are explicitly stated. The same is true for many public schools. But many school norms are not stated; instead they are conveyed implicitly, in a wide variety of ways. School routines—homeroom announcements, assemblies, pep rallies—and day-to-day interactions in classrooms, hallways, and gyms let students know who and what type of behavior is favored. Over the course of a school year, every student will witness thousands of incidents, and how teachers and principals respond—what they say and what they do not say—is indicative of approval, disapproval, or indifference to various kinds of behavior.

The World We Created at Hamilton High, by Gerald Grant, reveals the inner workings of the high school where the riots took place. His account, along with other accounts, gives the background observations for our theory. It reveals how the teachers and principal related to each other and to the students and how the students interacted. We see how norms and ideals were conveyed.

In the 1950s and early 1960s, Hamilton High was the picture of a white middle-class American high school. The principal viewed his job as "enforcing middle-class standards of courtesy and respect, emphasizing a college preparatory curriculum and putting winning teams on the Hamilton field."[4] The typical student was engaged in school activities such as the newspaper, Greek-letter fraternities and sororities, the girls' club, and the a capella chorus.

In 1969, this all changed. A court order forced the city to integrate its schools, and a significant number of poor black students were bused in. Daily clashes began almost immediately. Black students and their parents accused the white students and the staff of racism and unfair application of school rules. Grant illustrates how perceived slights could be overt as well as subtle. He presents the following interaction between a teacher and a black student as a typical classroom exchange:

> *Teacher* (to black student): Please sit down and stop talking.
> *Student:* I was only seeing if I could borrow a pencil and a piece of paper for that quiz you were talking about.
> *Teacher:* You know you're supposed to be in your seat.
> *Student:* But you will give me a zero if I don't have a quiz paper.
> *Teacher* (slightly exasperated): Sit down. You're supposed to bring those things to class or borrow them before class.
> *Student* (voice rising): Why you picking on me? You don't pick on white kids who borrow a piece of paper.[5]

Tensions rose between students and teachers and between the white and black students. The riots began after a fraternity party behind the school, where white students told a group of blacks to "get out of our school." The next Monday, some of the new students tore up the school cafeteria. Reflecting back some time later, a chemistry teacher summarized students' feelings: "The black students were responding to the way they were being treated. You know, it's like these white teachers don't really care anything about me. . . . He isn't teaching me anything. You know, it's a handout sheet every day or it's a film every day. The teacher may be making racist remarks, overt or subtle." The principal of the school at the time later summed it up: "[The school] gave them the message that they didn't belong."[6]

While court-ordered busing created the world at Hamilton High, research starting with August Hollingshead's *Elmtown's Youth* and James Coleman's *Adolescent Society* shows that student groups are ubiquitous in United States high schools.[7] Adolescents sort themselves into such groups, and their group norms become the ideals of their school society.[8] Coleman writes that the social structures of the schools are an image of adult society— but a distorted one, like "a Coney Island mirror."[9] The racial divisions of Hamilton High are such distortions of the adult social structure.

Coleman used clever interview techniques to elicit from students the norms in different schools—inquiring about what was required to belong to the "leading crowd." *Jocks and Burnouts*, Penelope Eckert's later ethnographic study, shows how these norms manifested themselves in the hallways and in the classrooms in a high school outside Detroit. The two groups behaved in very different ways, along many different dimensions. Jocks wore pastels; burnouts wore dark colors. Burnouts smoked; jocks abstained. Jocks hung out around the lockers and avoided the courtyard; burnouts avoided the lockers and hung out in the courtyard.[10] One difference between the groups stands out as fundamental: the jocks accepted the school's authority, whereas the burnouts rejected it. We emphasize this difference in our theory.

A recent paper by John Bishop and Michael Bishop takes these observations one step further.[11] They observe that students who challenge the leading crowd are teased and bullied. Students are especially vulnerable because they want to be popular, and that requires acceptance by the leading crowd.[12] And the very dominance of the leading crowd allows it to occupy key spaces that others must physically pass through. In Eckert's school, the jocks dominated the locker area in the main corridors of the school, while the burnouts skulked off to the courtyard.[13]

Why do the burnouts behave this way? Another classic school ethnography, Paul Willis's *Learning to Labour*, seeks to answer that question.[14] From 1972 to 1975, Willis studied a school in England. To Willis, the school itself, as an institution, embodies a set of norms. These norms are conveyed by the teachers, who value order and discipline. These norms are also conveyed by the administration, which sponsors programs to "reform" working-class youth. Willis followed a group of teenagers in their day-to-day activities, in and out of school. His account shows their reactions to such school messages. The group he followed called themselves the "lads." They contrasted themselves to the "ear'oles," who just sat still and listened, as they were told to do. The lads constantly broke school rules. They drank, smoked, disrupted class, and especially liked generating a "laff" (playing a nasty practical joke). Their clothes suggested sexual maturity, just as smoking and drinking indicated their rejection of school rules meant for children. On the day before graduation, the lads got drunk at a pub at lunchtime and returned to school. The school authorities refused to let them graduate. The teachers wondered why the lads had not waited until the evening for their spree, so that they could at least have graduated. But that failure to understand reflects the different ideals of the school staff and the lads. Had the boys waited until evening, the spree would not have served its purpose—as the lads' last laff.

Other ethnographies show us that these lads are not unique. Douglas Foley, who studied a high school in West Texas, relates a similar story about Mexican-American teens.[15] He hitched a ride with some *vatos* to an away football game.[16] The boys lit up joints on the way and discussed their plans to chase the local girls and provoke a fight with the local young men. They aimed to subvert a "respectable event to be disrespectful, rebellious and cool."[17] Just as the lads used their school's rules against alcohol and smoking as the context for their displays, the *vatos* used their school's preoccupation with football as the backdrop for their behavior.

Willis and Foley see it as no coincidence that the lads and the *vatos* come from working-class families. To these teenagers, the schools are insulting. The only *vato* who made it into the middle class talked to Foley, ten years later, about his high school experience. He talked of his and his friends' anger at the school and at the teachers, and of the social divisions in the school: "We were really angry about the way the teachers treated us. They looked down on us and never really tried to help us. A lot of us were real smart kids, but we never figured that the school was going to do anything for us. . . . We were the violent macho types, I guess. They'd [the teachers] manipulate the nerds into school and books. There was a real separation between us and the nerds and the jocks."[18]

An Identity Model of Students and Schools

Following these observations, we use our procedure from Chapter 3 to build an elementary theory of students and schools. As before, we start with a boilerplate economic model and add our three identity ingredients.

The Procedure: Part 1. In the boilerplate model, a student faces the economic costs and benefits of education. The costs include the cost of exerting effort on schoolwork, as well as foregone wages and any other expenses. The benefits are higher future wages.

The Procedure: Part 2.

Social Categories. How do students identify themselves? Following the title of Eckert's study, we suppose that there are two social categories: *jocks* and *burnouts*. In the terminology we used in our analysis of organizations, we could also call them insiders and outsiders. Of course, studies of schools describe many more categories, and also a residual category for students who do not fit, or choose not to fit, into any one group. Adding such complications to our analysis would not change its basic conclusions.

In this model, students have different characteristics, such as different parental income and athletic ability. Given their characteristics, students choose their groups.

Norms and Ideals. Jocks should be good-looking, wear appropriate clothes, and, for boys, be athletic. Burnouts should be and should do the opposite of jocks. They should wear different clothes from the jocks and eschew athletics. As for schoolwork, a jock should exert some effort in school (but not as much as *nerds,* who would be a third category in an expanded version of this theory). Burnouts are supposed to do very little schoolwork.

Gains and Losses in Identity Utility. Because jocks have higher social status, a student has a higher identity utility simply by being a jock. But this identity utility depends on how well the individual student fits the jock ideal. A student who does not fit the group's norms but who still tries to do so (what kids sometimes call a "wannabe") suffers a loss. Students also gain or lose identity utility insofar as the effort they put in departs from their ideal. Thus jocks lose utility if they do too much or too little schoolwork. Burnouts lose utility from putting in more than minimal effort.

The solution to the model gives the decisions of students— whether to be a jock or a burnout, and whether to work hard in school—and the decisions of school administrators to change the norms and ideals. Students face a key trade-off. When choosing between jock and burnout, students will balance the gains of a jock identity, which includes economic rewards, against the identity losses from trying to fit in. There are different ideals for how jocks and burnouts should behave. That choice is then a determinant of effort in school.

Although we have said that students make a "choice" between being a jock or a burnout, our model allows for this choice to be very much limited. For example, students who physically or socially do not correspond to the jock image usually find it hard to fit in. Students from different ethnic or racial backgrounds may not fit the ideal, no matter how much they would like to. Students who cannot fit the jock ideal have two bad choices: they may choose to be jocks and suffer the consequences of not really fitting in, or they may become burnouts.

Our model indicates, first, that the economic return to education (higher wages, more pleasant jobs) can be a weak determinant of students' efforts in school. The identity elements can be paramount. When the jock ideal is difficult to meet, more students choose to be burnouts. They exert too little effort relative to the economic optimum, and increases in future wages will have only a modest effect. Hence the model clearly captures the phenomenon of teenagers who do not apply themselves in school. Burnouts also drop out earlier, forgoing the large potential economic benefits.

The solution to the model also describes the effects of key choices of school administrators. Administrators might be able to influence what it means to be a jock. They may influence the insider ideal for example, by supporting athletic programs or other activities. Administrators also face a trade-off. They can try to alter the ideals so that students who identify with the school will exert more effort in schoolwork, resulting in higher academic standards and more learning for those who fit in. But such pressures also mean that more students may rebel and become burnouts.

The Model and Evidence: From Hamilton High to Shopping Mall High

The validity of this model is borne out by studies of schools, and thus this theory brings us closer to an understanding of student motivation and education.

At Hamilton High, the disruption of the school is exactly what the model predicts. The problems at Hamilton High are an extreme version of the day-to-day struggle to maintain school order. Richard Everhart, along with Willis, Foley, Lois Weiss, and others, paints a remarkably similar picture of the many small and large ways students assert themselves against teachers' authority, disrupting class and school operations.[19] When students do not identify with the school and accept its authority, learning does not occur.

At Hamilton High, the school administration, before the influx of new students, had adjusted its ideal to balance the trade-off between academic achievement and students becoming burnouts. That ideal may have been appropriate for the old pre-busing student population; it was inappropriate for the new. The black students did not fit the ideal of the school. Rather than try and become jocks, they became burnouts and disrupted the school. It was closed sporadically, for months at a time, over a period of years.

As the school adjusted to its newly diverse student body, it changed along the lines our model would predict. The Greek-letter clubs and the a capella choruses faded away. A new school emerged, defined by tolerance and students' rights to choose.

At Hamilton High, as in other schools throughout the country, students in the 1970s were granted greater rights. Gone were the days of the teacher's unquestioned right to act in loco parentis and a consensus on the school's ideals. New rules essentially eliminated teachers' authority to enforce academic and other behavioral standards. Arbitration guidelines adopted in 1972 allowed students to initiate grievance procedures "when the behavior of any staff member willfully imposes upon a student the ethical, social or political values of the staff member."[20] Teachers only rarely corrected student behavior, inside or outside the classroom. When a teacher asked a habitually tardy student for a note of explanation, a parent responded: "Stop worrying my child just because you have a middle-class hang-up about time."[21] Teachers had to defend their allegations about cheating and other student infractions to the principal, to parents, and even, on occasion, to lawyers.

Students gained the right to choose their curriculum. The school instituted more elective courses; only ten of the eighteen credits required for graduation were required courses. Even though formal academic tracking was eliminated, students now tracked themselves. Those interested in academics sought out the best teachers, and others chose less challenging courses. As the school adopted more laissez-faire policies, the troubles died down. Learning took root again, but the previous standards no longer applied.

This new school, as described by Grant, has been likened to the composite picture of the American high school presented by Arthur Powell and his coauthors in *The Shopping Mall High School*. The high school of the 1980s and 1990s that they portray is arguably not just the result of social changes in the 1960s, like Hamilton High.[22] It is also the outcome of continuing democratization of U.S. schools that began earlier in the century. One aspect of this change was the introduction of "life skills" curricula for non–college-bound students, who were said to be "preparing for life."[23]

Our model yields a picture of this new Shopping Mall High School. In an expansion of the model we described, the school can choose not to impose a uniform ideal. Instead, like shoppers at the mall, students get to choose the ideals they want. If you want to be a bandie, there is the band; if you want to be a nerd, there are the advanced placement classes and the chess club; and if you want to learn nothing at all, there are classes for that, too. Powell and his coauthors give examples of teachers who have implicitly signed a treaty with their students: "I don't teach, and you don't learn." These classes pass the time and are, sometimes, a bit of fun. By giving students choice, the school allows more students to feel like insiders and thus avoids disruption.

Shopping Mall High School may or may not be a happy place, but it is definitely an irresponsible one. In the view of most educational reformers, the duty of the high school is not to give students what they want: its duty is to tell them what they need. The public high schools, according to this critique, instead, take the existing goals of their students as their own. Most students put too low a value on academic achievement. The education critics think that this is the single leading reason for the mediocrity of U.S. schools. As evidence, they cite the poor performance of American schools in comparative international tests.

Miracle Schools and School Reform

A handful of schools have been widely studied as successful examples of different types of school reform. We test our model further by seeing how well these schools, which are so unusual and special, fit our model of what makes schools successful or unsuccessful.

Let's begin with the reforms at New York City's Central Park East Elementary Schools and Secondary School. There is no doubt about the schools' success. In East Harlem, a neighborhood where eighteen-year-old men are more likely to go to jail than to college, the high school (CPESS) has almost no dropouts; it sends 90 percent of its graduates on to college.[24] These differences from neighboring schools are so large that they cannot be explained by the selection bias of unusually concerned parents.

Accounts suggest that success lies in students' and teachers' identification with the school and its academic ideals. This identification is no accident. From the very beginning, school administrators set out to create a new type of school with a strong sense of community. The schools provide students a sanctuary in their dysfunctional neighborhoods and isolate them in a different social world. The importance of creating a new social category is apparent to Deborah Meier, the schools' founder, who claims: "We committed ourselves openly and loudly to being different."[25]

The unusual pedagogy and arrangements underlie the group identity of the schools. The curriculum is generated by the ideas of students themselves. In CPESS, they examine their ideas systematically using the "Five Habits of Mind." These five habits require asking and answering the questions: "How do we know what we know?" "Who's speaking?" "What causes what?" "How might things have been different?" and "Who cares?"[26] The school's other practices help students identify with each other and the school. It is small overall and has small classes. Its class structure is designed to encourage familiarity between students and teachers. Teachers stay with the same class of students for more than one academic year, and in the higher grades, unlike the specialist teachers at most high schools, they teach more than one subject to the same students. Instruction emphasizes student ideas and student presentations and projects as well as lengthy, open-ended teacher-parent conferencing: all these measures are designed to make all students feel as if they belong, as if to a family.

James Comer's *School Power* describes another example of identity-based school reform.[27] Comer describes the situation when he arrived at Baldwin Elementary, in a blighted area of New Haven, Connecticut, as "shocking." The teachers were unable to establish order. Children milled around: they yelled, they screamed; they called the teacher and each other names.[28] Five years later, under Comer's direction, order reigned. The cover of *School Power* shows a classroom with all students neatly dressed. They are at their desks, all smiling, with raised hands.[29]

Comer says he knew his program was a success when he saw a student stop a fight on the playground with the words: "We don't do that in this school."[30] The child had learned that there is a *we* with which students identified, and associated that group with norms for their school. How was this identity achieved? Comer worked with all four constituencies of the school—students, teachers, administrators, and parents—to ensure that each understood the goals of the others. He realized, as is borne out by the observations of Willis, Foley, and others, that much of the anger against a school may come from social divisions in the outside adult world. Comer therefore worked hard to encourage parent participation. Teachers scheduled extensive consultations with the parents of each child to help them understand that the teachers were the allies, not the enemies, of their children.

The disciplinary process at Baldwin was also designed to foster the internalization of school values, as the handling of an angry fifth grader illustrates. The boy was being disciplined for attacking a smaller child with his belt. Rather than simply punish the student who misbehaved, the teacher, who had been trained to look for causes of misbehavior, wormed out of the boy that he was upset because his father had been denied a pass from jail for Christmas. She helped him write a letter to his father. But at the same time, she made him understand that his problems did not entitle him to take out his feelings on other children.[31] That is, children were taught not only how to read, but also that they should obey the rules. In contrast to the passivity of Shopping Mall High, the Comer program actively promotes an identity and norms that value learning and the school.

Some would describe Core Knowledge schools at the opposite end of the school-reform spectrum. But we will see that their method is actually similar. In these schools the curriculum is the "core knowledge" that the education reformer Donald Hirsch says everyone should have. The curriculum is used as the unifying concept that "promotes a community of learners—for adults and children."[32] The structured approach to knowledge is associated with similarly strict attitudes toward other aspects of comportment. At the Parker (Colorado) Core Knowledge Charter School, a stringent dress code is enforced: it even stipulates that socks "must be worn in a coordinated color with the school uniform, and worn in a matching pair of the same color." Discipline is similarly strict: students and parents must sign an agreement to abide by the school's code.[33] This is another example of the way in which discipline defines communities.[34]

While the Core Knowledge pedagogy is opposite from those of CPESS and Theodore Sizer's affiliated Coalition for Essential Schools, all are based on the same theory of motivation. Successful schools actively engineer their students' identities and norms. One type of school tells students that they should be disciplined, from the mastering of a structured curriculum to the matching of their socks. The other tells students that they should be independent thinkers, from the execution of individual projects to the systematic practice of the Five Habits of Mind. In each case, though in a different way, the schools have taken responsibility for telling students who they are and how they should behave. CPESS does so by creating a feeling of the school itself as family. At Baldwin Elementary, Comer relates how he worked to create the same feelings by working with all four of the school's major constituencies. And because identity is closely linked to dress and self-presentation, we consider it no coincidence that a Core Knowledge school might prescribe even the nature of a student's socks.

The descriptions of these schools and how they operate do not explain in detail why they were able to achieve their goals. They mainly tell what they did and why (we may be greedy in asking for more), but they do not tell us what was going through the minds of the students. But Coleman, followed by Bishop and Bishop, would suggest an explanation for why these reforms worked so well: the changes in expectations for the students in the classroom, and perhaps elsewhere, had a secondary effect. They changed how the members of the leading crowds thought they should behave. This in turn affected how students behaved toward each other—including who was, or was not, teased and bullied.

Private versus Public Schools

Our theory also captures key differences between private and public schools in the United States. The authors of *Shopping Mall High* and many other critics of U.S. education have derided the public schools because they fail to teach their students how they should behave. In contrast, Anthony Bryk and his co-authors quote a school philosophy statement from the Catholic schools. It describes their clarity of expectations: A student "should be marked by a number of characteristics: . . . intellectually competent, . . . loving, . . . a person of faith, . . . [and] committed to doing justice."[35] Each of the desirable characteristics is described in detail.

What arrangements foster these norms? The teachers collectively assume responsibility for shaping student character. The ideal Catholic schoolteacher is supposed to be involved in many aspects of students' lives.[36] The English teacher of the morning is likely to be the counselor at lunch time or possibly the soccer coach of the afternoon.[37] Wide participation in school activities, including a greater fraction of students participating on athletic teams and shared religious activities, foster the sense of community. Such community affects the ideals of the leading crowds and also counteracts their ability to bully others.

Do Catholic schools do a better job of educating students? We cannot be sure, of course, because the parents who send their children to Catholic schools may be different from other parents in ways a statistician cannot observe. We do know that students from Catholic schools are much less likely to drop out and much more likely to go on to a four-year college. A study by Joseph Altonji, Todd Elder, and Christopher Taber tried to account for selection bias by studying a sample of students who were in Catholic schools in the eighth grade, some of whom continued to Catholic high schools and some of whom switched to public schools.[38] In all observable respects, the two groups were similar before they entered high school. But those who continued in the Catholic schools had a considerably greater chance of graduating and attending college.[39]

The raw statistics from their sample paint the picture well. Fifteen percent of those who had switched to public school by the tenth grade became dropouts, compared to only 2 percent of those who had remained in the Catholic schools. Similar differences apply to an urban minority subsample.[40] It seems that once the Catholic schools have got you, they do not let you go until you graduate.[41]

Race and Schooling

Racial differences have already been featured in this chapter. Three statistics indicate the depth of the racial fault line in American education. Black students are 50 percent more likely to drop out of high school than whites.[42] They are 40 percent less likely to obtain a bachelor's degree.[43] In the standard national achievement test (the National Assessment of Educational Progress), the median math and reading scores for blacks are almost a full standard deviation less than the median scores for whites.[44] Why are these gaps so large and so persistent?

The standard economic models of education suggest three reasons. First, if African-American students with the same skills earn lower wages than whites, they have less incentive to work hard in school.[45] Second, if schools in African-American neighborhoods have fewer resources, then the students again have less incentive to work hard in school. A student may work hard, but if the chemistry laboratory has no equipment, it is difficult to learn the scientific method. Third, historically, African-American parents have been educationally deprived, which makes it more difficult to help their children academically.

All three of these factors play a role in this gap. But close observation of what goes on in the schools suggests that there is a fourth reason. School routines and curricula often convey to black students that there is something wrong with them and their background. Lisa Delpit gives one telling, subtle example, regarding how teachers' presumption of the superiority of standard English can (inadvertently) insult African-American children. In a reading lesson, a girl renders the text "Yesterday I washed my brother's clothes" as "Yesterday I wash my bruvver close." The teacher corrects her. But the student has done something far more sophisticated than read: she has translated the passage into her own dialect. Instead of being praised, the girl is told that she has made a mistake.[46]

Another incident is less subtle. But it captures, again in microcosm, the type of interaction that, repeated again and again, is almost certain to make African-American students feel that there is a difference between *us* and the *them* who run the schools. Berkeley, California, is one of the most liberal and, in some respects, one of the most racially integrated cities in the United States. Ann Ferguson's participant-observer study of a Berkeley middle school is therefore especially revealing.[47] This school mixes two populations: upper-income, mainly white and Asian students from the Hills and lower-income, mainly black and Hispanic students from the Flats. The kids from the Flats and those from the Hills do not share the same understanding of appropriate comportment. Teachers and school administrators, who feel it is part of their job to maintain order, mainly share Hill standards of behavior: they label the kids from the Flats as "bad" and punish them harshly.

As an example, Ferguson narrates the following incident, which would be comic if the frequent repetition of such incidents did not make it instead deeply tragic. Ferguson is on the stairs talking to the vice principal when he is distracted by a group of minority girls talking loudly as they pass by between classes. One of the children fails to notice him and keeps talking. The vice principal asks her, "Is this how you are supposed to behave in the halls?" and then commands her to retrace her steps, down the stairs and up again. The girl does so primly, but also with just a hint of humor. The vice principal perceives this behavior as disrespectful (as it may have been) and sends her to his office for the day.[48] What is happening here? In our earlier language, the vice principal, as an insider with the mission of making the school orderly, does not see the humor in a student who challenges that order by asserting, even if just for a moment, that she is an outsider who does not fully respect his authority.

Ferguson thinks that a white child would have been treated differently: the vice principal would have not have seen the loud chatter as disorderly. A white child, who fits better the school insider ideal, would have been less likely to be cheeky in response. And the vice principal would have been less likely to deal out a severe punishment. With a white child he considered an insider, he might even have perceived the same cheekiness as funny. Is he really punishing the girl because he thinks that she is asserting herself as an outsider? Who knows? Such minor misunderstandings happen routinely in this school.

Is it hard to believe that such incidents affect students' feelings about their school and shape the norms of the leading crowds? We cannot be sure that such incidents produce an "oppositional culture" among black students; but we do know that the performance gap between black and white students is large, and our prisons hold a disproportionate number of young African Americans. More specifically, we also know that Berkeley High is marked by racial tension and parts of the school have even been deliberately burned down.

Our theory regarding how schools can deal with diversity also suggests a resolution to a curious empirical paradox. If black students are angered by school culture, we might think they have less favorable attitudes toward school than white students. But evidence suggests the contrary. Philip Cook and Jens Ludwig show that, compared to non-Hispanic whites, blacks have about the same expectations for educational attainment (graduation from high school, college, and so on) and about the same school attendance and effort.[49] We tabulated students' answers to some of the questions in the U.S. Department of Labor's *High School and Beyond* random-sample survey. These tabulations show that black students in fact have better attitudes toward school than white students. On average, compared to whites, blacks are less likely to "dread" English or math class, more likely to perceive school spirit as "excellent," more likely to report a "positive attitude toward self," and much more likely to "like working hard in school."[50] These findings seem paradoxical in view of the large and persistent gap between black and white test scores.

Our theory gives a possible explanation why blacks appear to have better attitudes toward school than whites but, nevertheless, have lower test scores. Blacks and whites, by and large, attend different schools. Schools adjust their curricula and their ideals to their respective student bodies. Should the students read Ernest Hemingway or Toni Morrison? It is likely that schools with a majority black (or white) student population will adapt to their students' tastes. As a consequence, black students might be more likely to "dread" English class and math class in predominantly white schools than in predominantly black schools, with the reverse being true for white students. Our tabulations showed such a pattern exactly. Blacks in almost totally white schools were, indeed, more likely to dread English and math than their counterparts in all-black schools.[51] Symmetrically, white students in almost totally black schools were more likely to dread English; they also were somewhat more likely to dread math relative to their peers at all-white schools (although this result was not statistically significant).[52]

Identity Economics and the Demand and Supply of Education

The Demand for Education. In this chapter we focus on student motivations. Economists have long understood that students have nonpecuniary motives. Identity economics forces us to specify what those motives might be and gives us a series of questions to bring them to life. How does a student think of herself within the school—what is her social category? What does she think she should do in school—what are her norms and what is her ideal? And what losses are entailed if she deviates from those norms? The answers to these questions play a major role in determining the demand for education, that is, how long students stay in school. Because schooling is a major determinant of future earnings, the demand for education ultimately determines both the level and the distribution of income.

The Supply of Education. Most formal education takes place in schools, which are one form of organization. The previous chapter tells us that the identity and motivations of teachers and administrators are also keys to the success of a school. Thus identity economics also gives a better understanding of the supply of education. From what we see inside schools, it is not just the level of resources allocated to schools that determines the effective supply, but also the use of those resources.

Much attention has been devoted to teacher quality, for example. Steven Rivkin, Eric Hanushek, and John Kain, in a follow-up to Hanushek's earlier work, found that student learning differs greatly depending on the student's teacher.[53] Using a large data set from Texas with students matched to teachers, they saw that some teachers were consistently much more effective than others. They conclude not only that high-quality teachers are critical for educational attainment, but also that the test-score gap between high- and low-income students could be substantially reduced if low-income students had better teachers.[54] Our analysis suggests one possible reason for their finding that teachers matter: some teachers may be more effective in running their classrooms so that students identify with them and the school. The same is true for administrators, of course. Deborah Meier and James Comer were not effective simply because they found some miracle cure for low student achievement. They and their staffs were also unusually effective in changing students' self-conceptions. In this sense, the miracles they fostered occurred with abundant resources, used in a particular way.

Of course, the miracles also depend on teachers' and administrators' identification with the school and its mission. In CPESS, the teachers and principal identify with the goals of the school— goals that they created. The committed Catholic school teachers and administrators described by Anthony Bryk and colleagues contrast with the typical disengaged teacher in *Shopping Mall High*. Thus the extent to which teachers identify with their school's mission may be as important as differences in student motivation in explaining the gap between Catholic and public schools. Drawing from the lessons in the previous chapter, a teacher who views himself as an insider will engage in higher effort, but a teacher who feels like an outsider, like Mike in Studs Terkel's account, will put in low effort and may create problems for other teachers and the school administration.

Identity, School Goals, and School Choice

Reflecting our own bias as economists, we have presumed that a school's goal is to maximize students' skills and future incomes. But instilling skills is only one of the goals of schools and of the parents who choose them. Religious schools, for example, often eschew economic goals in favor of religious goals. A school's primary mission may be the separation of the saved from the damned, as suggested by the principal in Allen Peshkin's ethnography of Bethany Baptist School: "The devil's crowd is after our kids."[55] A similar desire for separation lay behind the voucher-supported private academies established (unconstitutionally) in the wake of *Brown v. Board of Education of Topeka, Kansas.*[56] The goals and curricula of public schools are the product of elected school boards: the nature of these schools, their ideals, may therefore derive from the political economy of a community. Charter schools also appeal to particular communities within a jurisdiction. Home schools, of course, are the ultimate tailored school setting.

These examples all suggest that identity and school goals play a major role in the debate over school choice. But even on the narrow question of whether school choice leads to greater student skill, identity is central. Parents will choose schools according to the school's mission, so that a high proportion of students in such schools will be insiders. And insiders will have higher achievement to the extent that achievement is promoted by the school.

Part Three

Gender and Race

SEVEN

Gender and Work

ONLY 7 PERCENT OF nurses in the United States are men. There are so few men in nursing that people use the phrase "male nurse" to describe one. The phrase not only describes a statistical anomaly; it also reveals a social contradiction that people recognize and discuss. In the movie *Meet the Parents,* it is a cause for consternation when the daughter brings home a male nurse as her prospective husband. There are advocacy groups for men in nursing; *Male Nursing Magazine* promotes "male-friendly" nursing schools and offers tips on how to navigate the female-dominated profession.

Regarding the predominance of men or women, nursing is not the exception but the rule. By and large, men and women in the United States work in different occupations. Occupational segregation is one of the most stubborn features of the American labor market. From the early 1900s until as recently as 1970, two-thirds of women (or men) in the United States would have had to change jobs to equalize gender distribution in occupations. Between 1970 and 1990, occupational segregation declined, but in 1990 still more than half (53 percent) of men or women would have had to switch jobs in order to achieve an equal distribution.[1]

What can explain the existence of and trends in occupational segregation? Economists have studied women and men in the labor market for decades. Identity economics takes the next step and enhances our current theories—of comparative advantage, taste-based discrimination, and statistical discrimination, which we describe below. Identity accounts for trends in occupational segregation and allows us to evaluate policy. In particular, we can study the full spectrum of sex-discrimination law.

The heart of our theory is again the distinction between norms and garden-variety tastes. Individual workers may like certain kinds of work, be particularly adept at a task, or have a particular talent in a specific field. But in our theory, certain jobs are deemed appropriate for women and others for men. These are occupational norms. Around 1970, for example, the norms stipulated that men *should* be breadwinners, working in such professions as construction, engineering, and accounting; women, if they worked, *should* be nurses, teachers, and secretaries.

Our identity model comes from observation. Researchers have studied law firms, hospitals, factories, and shop floors; the ways people describe their work and how they feel about their jobs; and the ways they react to those who enter nontraditional professions.

Jobs have tags. There are men's jobs and women's jobs.[2] Thus, *female nuclear engineer* and *female marine* seem contradictory, as do *male nurse* and *male secretary*. These designations have been justified, in part, by the presumed qualities of men and women. Women have been thought to be "nurturing" and "patient," qualities that suit them for positions as elementary school teachers and nurses; back in the days when spinning was a significant occupation, they were thought to have "nimble fingers." In contrast, qualities associated with men make them suitable for positions as administrators, doctors, and pilots.

Whether or not such suitability is based on real differences, these associations affirm stereotypes of what men and women should do. Thus, for example, the view that women are biologically less fit for jobs in science and engineering is not just an innocent hypothesis to be checked by able statisticians. Such statements are part of the penumbra that tags such occupations as jobs for men. They reinforce a social code that has kept generations of women out of careers in science. Whatever the biological differences may be, the mere presumption that differences exist gives an economic rationale for what is called statistical discrimination, which, as we shall see later, is illegal.

Rhetoric surrounding shifts of certain jobs from male- to female-dominated further demonstrates the salience of gender and job associations. To make socially acceptable the recruitment of women into traditionally male jobs during World War II, for example, it was accompanied by official propaganda and popular literature picturing women taking on factory work without loss of femininity.[3] In addition, it was the wartime emergency that excused the violation of the usual gender prescriptions.

Ethnographic studies indicate that people continue to view some jobs as appropriate for men and others for women. Those who violate these norms are often ambivalent about their work and subject to harassment and even violence. The anthropologist Jennifer Pierce spent fifteen months working as a paralegal at a San Francisco Bay Area law firm in the early 1990s and recorded how conceptions of male and female jobs played out in the workplace.[4] The female lawyers wanted to think of themselves as women, but they faced a dilemma. Being a good lawyer meant acting "like a man." It meant being "like Rambo," "taking no prisoners," "winning big," and "having balls." In a Christmastime skit, a male partner, Michael, is portrayed as comfortable in his authority. In contrast, a female partner portrayed in the skit, Rachel, is unable to make up her mind whether "to be a man or a woman."[5]

Many writers document the harassment women face when they work in "men's" jobs. Men sometimes react violently to their female co-workers. Such reactions reveal emotions beyond the simple dislike for working with women that has been posited in earlier theories of discrimination. The sociologist Irene

85

Padavic provides a firsthand account from her job as a coal han-
dler in a large utility company.[6] After only a short stay, her male
co-workers picked her up bodily, tossed her back and forth, and
attempted to push her onto the coal conveyor belt. The men
said it was just a joke.

The harassment lawsuit against Eveleth Mines in Minnesota
offers further graphic details. In August 1988, the employees
Lois Jenson and Patricia Kosmach filed a class-action suit against
Eveleth under Title VII of the Civil Rights Act. They charged
that the company was liable for the harassment they faced from
co-workers after they and other women started working in the
mines. The case worked its way through three levels of the courts.
The Court of Appeals summarized the women's testimony:

> Sexually explicit graffiti and posters were found on the walls
> and in lunchroom areas, tool rooms, lockers, desks, and of-
> fices. Such material was found in women's vehicles, on eleva-
> tors, in women's restrooms, in inter-office mail, and in locked
> company bulletin boards. . . . Women reported incidents of
> unwelcome touching, including kissing, pinching, and grab-
> bing. Women reported offensive language directed at indi-
> viduals as well as frequent "generic" comments that women
> did not belong in the mines, kept jobs from men, and be-
> longed home with their children. . . . Some male employees
> subjected female employees to physical conduct of a sexual
> nature. In one incident, a male employee pretended to per-
> form oral sex on a sleeping female co-worker.[7]

At one point in the proceedings, even the defense conceded
unequal treatment. But it argued that Eveleth was not guilty because the treatment was due to the larger "culture of the Iron
Range mining industry." The court, unimpressed, awarded
punitive damages. Eventually, the company, facing an appeal
and the prospect of another jury trial, settled out of court for
$3.5 million.[8]

An Identity Model of the Labor Market

On the basis of these observations, we build a theory of gender in
the workplace. We again follow the procedure from Chapter 3.

We specify a standard economic model of the labor market. We then posit workers' utility functions with three identity ingredients. In these utility functions, workers have a sense of who they are in society and how they and others should behave. Here, workers' utility reflects gender categories and norms.

The Procedure: Part 1. We start with a boilerplate model of a labor market. There are firms that desire to hire workers to do tasks—yielding the demand for labor. There are men and women who desire to work—yielding the supply of labor. Some men and women are better at a task than others, with no overall difference between men and women. A boilerplate labor market model would stop here. Solving for the wage where supply equals demand yields the number of men and women employed.

The Procedure: Part 2. We add our three identity ingredients.

Social Categories. The social categories are simply *men* and *women*.

Norms and Ideals. Some tasks are labeled appropriate for men —*men's jobs*. Other tasks are labeled *women's jobs*.

Gains and Losses in Identity Utility. Women lose utility from working in a man's job. And men lose utility from working in a woman's job. Men also lose utility when a woman works in a man's job. They can also sabotage the work of women; this sabotage increases the perpetrator's utility but leads to lower productivity for everyone.

We solve the model, finding the wage where labor supply equals labor demand and finding the number of women and men working in different jobs.

Our basic conclusion is that employers will usually hire men for men's jobs and women for women's jobs. On average, the women who work in men's jobs have higher skills than the men. Despite the underuse of women's skills, this employment pattern maximizes firms' profits because they pay lower overall wages. Another option for firms is to completely segregate men and women and avoid any loss in productivity due to retaliation and work disruption. This strategy entails an inefficient mix of workers' skills, but because of the separation there is no loss in productivity from sabotage. Finally, no single competitive firm has an incentive to change the society-wide gender norms, because any advantage would be eroded by competition.

Theory and Evidence

Because our model is based on observation of social interactions in the workplace, it is no surprise that the conclusions of the model fit actual labor-market patterns.

In our model, as in the U.S. labor market, employment patterns reflect the stereotypes of "women's jobs." Women do often work in "women's" occupations. Secretaries (96.7 percent female in 2007) have often been called "office wives." Elements of sexuality are inscribed into the working relationship.[9] Secretaries are expected to serve their male bosses with deference and to be attentive to their personal needs.[10] The care of young children has also traditionally been seen as women's work. It should be no surprise that in 2007, 97.3 percent of preschool and kindergarten teachers and 80.9 percent of elementary and middle school teachers were female.[11] Nurses (93.0 percent female) are supposed to be compassionate and care for the sick, as well as to be deferential to (traditionally male) doctors.[12]

Identity Economics and New Conclusions

By adding gender norms, identity economics fleshes out theories of sex discrimination and leads to new conclusions concerning workplace discrimination and occupational segregation.

Several previous theories yield similar predictions for wages and women's employment. In the first such model, which grew out of Gary Becker's work on racial discrimination, some firm owners are said to have a "distaste" for employing women. In the slightly more complicated version, the firm owner has no personal distaste for women employees, but male workers do. The firm must then pay men higher wages for working with women. Every woman hired by such a firm thus increases the firm's costs, and so firms will hire fewer women. In a competitive marketplace, either the workers will pay for their prejudice in terms of lower wages or the firms that indulge their workers' tastes will be replaced by lower-cost firms that do not hire such discriminatory workers.

In the second theory of this genre, men and women have different preferences for working outside the home. Women, it is said, have "a lower attachment" to the labor force.[13] Because they will be in and out of the labor force, women invest less in education and skills, whose return is realized only insofar as they work. Women then end up in jobs where less investment is required, and occupational segregation thus arises.[14]

A third theory posits *statistical discrimination*. Employers often cannot assess the skills of any individual worker. They make hiring decisions based on the average skills in a population. When women are presumed—correctly so within the model—to have lower average skills, employers hire fewer women and at lower wages.

Identity augments economists' view of discrimination and occupational segregation. We posit a set of norms that dictate proper behavior for men and women. In our model, men do not have a general distaste for working with women. Their distaste is instead job-specific. This specification reflects an observation. All over the world, men and women work together. But they typically have different jobs: women are secretaries; men are executives.

Our model then leads to new conclusions. First, it gives another perspective on occupational segregation. Our model goes beyond saying that women acquire fewer skills: it says that women invest in skills for jobs that are appropriate for women. Hence, women go to graduate schools of education rather than to business schools. On a deeper level, women may have "a lower attachment to the labor market" because of wider gender norms. Women are supposed to stay at home and raise children. They are therefore supposed to move in and out of the labor force, whereas men are not.[15]

Second, an identity theory suggests why discrimination and occupational segregation persist despite competitive market forces. It suggests that the real problem is the norms that stipulate that men and women should do particular jobs, irrespective of their individual tastes and abilities. No one firm, acting on its own, has much incentive to change the society-wide norms. The cost would be too high relative to the benefits for the individual firm. Small, competitive firms would derive only a small fraction of the overall returns from changing gender norms that are society-wide. Indeed, we have seen exactly such an argument in the *Eveleth* defense.

According to this theory, then, society-wide changes are necessary to change gender norms. The complete remedy for discrimination is to remove gender tags from jobs. Both at home and in the workplace, this has been an aim of the Women's Movement. The model predicts many implications of such changes. Women's participation in the labor force will increase. Occupational segregation will decrease. Male and female tenure in any single occupation will converge. More women will work in what were previously seen as men's jobs, and more men will work in traditionally women's jobs. All these outcomes have been observed. The Women's Movement and changes in the law—not changes in competition Becker-style—have been responsible for the shift in labor market patterns since the 1960s.[16] Associations of specific jobs with gender have diminished, as reflected in changes in language, and the job composition has shifted dramatically. *Firemen* have become *firefighters; policemen* have become *police officers;* and *chairmen* have become simply *chairs.* Women now stay at jobs almost as long as men. In 1968 the median job tenure of employed women over twenty-five was 3.3 years lower than that of men; by 1998 the gap had narrowed to 0.4 years.[17] Changes in sex composition within occupations accounted for the major share of the decline in occupational segregation between 1970 and 1990.[18] According to the U.S. Census Bureau, of the forty-five occupations that were 0.0 percent female in 1970, only one (supervisors: brickmasons, stonemasons, and tile setters) was less than 1 percent female twenty years later.[19] Some incursions into male-dominated professions have been very large. In 1970 women were only 24.6 percent of auditors and accountants and only 4.5 percent of lawyers. Twenty years later, more than half of auditors and accountants (52.7 percent) were women. The fraction of women lawyers had increased more than fivefold (to 24.5 percent). Not only did the proportion of women in men's jobs increase, but so did the proportion of men in women's jobs (although less dramatically).[20]

Traditional supply and demand would tell us that market outcomes are determined by technology, market structure, and the utility and profit motives of individual consumers and firms. Of the three possible explanations for changes in the labor market gender distribution—technology, market structure, and utility and profit—elimination makes workers' utility the leading suspect. There was no dramatic change in technology or market structure sufficient to explain the increased mixing of men and women on the job.[21] Legal initiatives, discussed below, also reflect such changes in norms.

Sex-Discrimination Law

Sex-discrimination law in the United States derives from Title VII of the Civil Rights Act of 1964. This act made it unlawful for an employer to discriminate "against any individual . . . with respect to . . . compensation, terms, conditions . . . of employment [or to adversely] limit, segregate, or classify his employees . . . because of . . . sex."[22] At its most basic, this law prohibits the taste-based discrimination represented in Gary Becker's theory.[23] The courts have also interpreted Title VII as outlawing statistical discrimination by sex or criteria correlated with sex. In *Phillips v. Martin-Marietta,* the firm hired fewer women because management thought women were less likely to want to hold and keep a job: they would be more likely to leave the labor force because of family obligations. Such discriminatory hiring is economically rational from the firm's point of view and appears, as we have seen, in economic theories of statistical discrimination. The Supreme Court ruled in 1971 that it is illegal to discriminate in this way: it is illegal to treat individual women according to a group stereotype, even when on average women have attributes that make them undesirable employees.[24]

Our model, where sex discrimination occurs because jobs have gender associations, corresponds to a wider interpretation of Title VII. This interpretation is at the forefront of current legal debate and is supported by a number of precedents. In *Diaz v. Pan American World Airways,* the court outlawed sex bans in hiring.[25] The airline pleaded for their prohibition of male flight attendants because women were better at the "non-mechanical aspects of the job." This association of gender with the job was disallowed because feminine traits were deemed irrelevant to the "primary function or services offered."[26] *Price Waterhouse v. Hopkins,* discussed in our introduction, set a precedent for banning discrimination in promotions of workers already hired.[27]

Cases have also involved harassment of women in "men's" jobs. *Berkman v. City of New York* reinstated a woman firefighter who had been dismissed because of substandard work.[28] The court ruled that harassment by her male co-workers made it impossible for her to perform her job adequately.[29] Vicki Schultz and Katherine Franke have argued that any harassment derived from gender norms has discriminatory implications (as depicted in our model) and is thus a violation of Title VII.[30] Such expansive interpretation of a "hostile work environment" has been exceptional. *Jenson v. Eveleth Taconite Co,* mentioned above, was the first successful class-action lawsuit against a firm that did not stop sexual harassment in its workplace. Following the views of Catharine MacKinnon, judges have instead usually viewed coercive sexual advances as the essential element of sexual harassment.[31] The law is still in flux.

Gender, Labor Supply, and the Household

The labor market is just one arena where gender norms affect economic outcomes. Economists are also very interested in what goes on inside the home: how couples divide the household chores and child-raising tasks, and how they decide who should go to work and for how many hours.[32] Research has demonstrated that gender norms can significantly influence the division of labor and leisure, and theoretically, economists have long departed from the "unitary model" of the household, in which the couple simply maximizes joint utility. Shelley Lundberg and Robert Pollak, for example, build strategic-bargaining models of the ways couples split household output, where gender norms set fallback options.[33] We apply identity economics to the household to obtain fine predictions of who does what kind of work and how much.

A boilerplate model of the household would be a sort of "comparative-advantage" model. The partner who is relatively better at household chores will work at home, whereas the partner who is relatively better at earning an income will go out to work. This theory would predict a symmetric pattern of the division of work: whoever works more inside the home will work less outside the home.

But, as should be no surprise, this is not the observed pattern in the United States. Women, even when they work more hours outside the home and supply the majority of the income, do more of the housework. Men, on average, do at most one-third.

An identity model easily produces such an outcome. We take a boilerplate economic model and add social categories of men and women. According to traditional gender norms, women *should* do the housework. These norms still shape home life in America, as we will see presently. In an identity model, a woman or man will lose identity utility when performing a gender-inappropriate task. Thus, even when a woman provides most of the family's income, she will do more housework.

We have described some statistics showing this pattern, and we will describe more of them in a moment. But first let us look inside some households to see the expressions of the norms that drive our theory. Arlie Hochschild's *Second Shift* describes the division of housework among middle-class couples in the San Francisco Bay Area, interviewed from 1980 to 1988. Although these couples preserved a myth that they shared the work equally, few of them actually did, as the men did the "men's work" in the household (of which there was relatively little), and the women did the "women's work" (which was considerable). Hochschild gives the example of the Holts, who said they had found a way to share the housework equally. Evan, a furniture salesman, took care of the lower half of the house (the basement and his tools). His wife, Nancy, a full-time licensed social worker, took care of the upper half. Care of the family's biological life was subject to a similar "equal" division: she took care of the child, he took care of the dog.[34]

Hochschild's sample and our data analysis suggest that the Holts conform to a national pattern. We studied the shares of housework reported by married couples in the Panel Study of Income Dynamics as they relate to their shares of paid work.[35] The answers came from husbands' and wives' self-reported response to the question: "About how much time do you (your spouse) spend on housework in an average week? I mean time spent cooking, cleaning, and doing other work around the house?" The question intentionally excluded child care. As shown in the figure, starting from the right, when husbands do all the paid work, they contribute on average about 10 percent of housework. As men's share of outside work falls, their share of housework rises, but to no more than 37 percent. The presence of children of different ages makes a small difference to the division of labor. Similar results obtain in the relation between shares of income and husband's share of housework.[36]

Other sources reach similar conclusions. Using a different data set, the National Survey of Families and Households, the sociologists Noriko Tsuya, Larry Bumpass, and Minja Kim Choe have also found low elasticity (low responsiveness) in the relation of men's hours of housework to their wives' hours of outside work in the United States.[37] Surprisingly, also, this elasticity is not significantly greater in the United States than in Japan and Korea, where women's roles are commonly believed to be much more traditionally defined. However, Japanese husbands put in a mean of only 2.5 hours of housework per week, as compared to 12.6 for their Korean and 7.8 hours for their American counterparts.[38]

In addition, beyond the overall division of housework between husbands and wives, the tasks of men and women within the home are far from randomly distributed. Women do 75 percent of the hours of traditional "women's work" (such as cooking, laundry, and house cleaning) and men do 70 percent of the "men's work" (such as yard work and auto repair).[39]

Husbands' share of housework

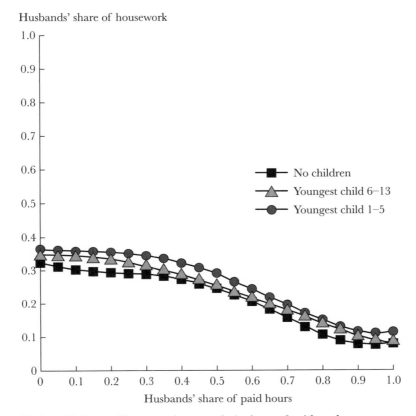

Husbands' share of paid hours

Husbands' share of housework versus their share of paid work.

Conclusion

The previous chapters show how adding identity enriches the current economics of organizations and education, and here we see how our method enriches the economics of gender. Specifically, gender norms tag tasks as male or female, both in the workplace and in the household. The models show us why it took a social movement and government intervention rather than a competitive marketplace to erode the discrimination against women in the United States.

EIGHT

Race and Minority Poverty

MINORITY POVERTY IS our last, but not least, extended application of identity economics in this book. Black/white disparities are arguably the United States' worst social problem. Their persistence is difficult to explain with current economic theories. With an identity model, the facts fall into place.

We ask why, despite the civil rights movement and programs such as affirmative action, so many African Americans still fare badly.

Since the civil rights movement, many African Americans have made significant economic gains. Between 1959 and 2001, the black poverty rate fell from 55 percent to 23 percent.[1] In 2001, more than half of African Americans had incomes more than double the poverty line. By these measures, there has been a burgeoning black middle class.[2]

But a continuing "American Dilemma" accompanies these gains.[3] Today roughly two-thirds of African-American children are born to single mothers, of whom almost three-fifths are in poverty.[4] At current rates, almost one-third of African-American men will spend some portion of their lives in prison.[5] Close to two-fifths of black men with a high school education or less are not employed during their prime working ages of 25 to 34.[6] They are out of the labor force, unemployed, or incarcerated. Among African-American high-school dropouts age 31 to 35, only 44 percent were at school or at work in 2000.[7]

A good theory of race and poverty should explain both the persistence of these disparities and the trends.

Traditional Economics of Discrimination

Two of the most prominent and respected economists in the world began the study of race discrimination in economics. We have already seen versions of these theories applied to gender. The first is Gary Becker's theory of *taste-based discrimination*. In this theory, white employers can dislike hiring black workers, and white workers can have a similar dislike of working with blacks. Whether it is the employers or employees who have these dislikes, the results are the same: black workers will receive less pay, and will work in different jobs, than whites.

Statistical discrimination, proposed by Kenneth Arrow, posits a different source of discrimination but yields similar results. In this theory, white employers discriminate against black employees, not because of their own desire to maintain physical or social distance, but instead because they think blacks, on average, have low skills. This can be a self-fulfilling prophecy: individual blacks have no incentive to acquire high skills because they will be judged as having low skills no matter what they do.[8]

Case studies show that overt discrimination still exists and thus may be part of the answer to our question. For example, studies show that employers, bankers, and car dealers treat African Americans differently from whites. Marianne Bertrand and Sendhil Mullainathan mailed in fictitious resumes in response to help-wanted ads.[9] The resumes for "Greg" and "Emily" (common names among whites) received 50 percent more requests for interviews than resumes for "Jamal" and "Lakisha" (common names among African Americans). Alicia Munnell and her coauthors found that a typical loan application that would have been rejected by a bank 28 percent of the time for an African-American applicant would have been rejected only 20 percent of the time for a white counterpart.[10] Ian Ayres and Peter Siegelman sent African-American and white men to get price quotations for a new car. The price quotes to African-American males were more than $1,000 higher than quotes to white males.[11]

While discrimination still exists, traditional theories cannot help us understand many patterns.[12] Many African Americans seem to choose courses of action that middle-class white and black Americans consider disastrous. For example:

- It is hard for traditional theory to explain out-of-wedlock birth rates that are more than two and a half times the rate for whites.[13]
- Traditional theory could explain the high incarceration rates if criminal activity is a better career path for African Americans than legal activities. But statistics indicate that crime does not pay. Steven Levitt and Sudhir Venkatesh studied the financial records of a Chicago gang. The typical "foot soldier" could have earned almost as much working for McDonald's, with much less risk.[14]
- It is a similar stretch for traditional theory to explain the low employment rates of African-American males. Other minority groups, such as Hispanics, have much higher rates of employment despite obstacles such as a lack of English skills.
- Yet more perplexing, if discrimination is to blame for these outcomes, why do we see a divergence in outcomes among African Americans? At the same time that the fraction of African Americans with middle-class incomes is increasing, there is also a rise in single-parent families, incarceration, and nonemployment.
- The economic theories are further confounded by the fact that the rate of return to skill acquisition for blacks is, if anything, higher than for whites.[15]

Basis for an Identity Theory

We need a better theory, and for that we turn to identity. Historically, there have been different codes for how blacks and whites should behave in America. Such a code was especially clear in the South and was formally reflected in Jim Crow laws. When Rosa Parks refused to give up her bus seat to a white man, she was arrested and fined. When the writer Richard Wright tried to train for a skilled job as an optometrist and lens grinder, the other employees threatened him, and he was forced to quit. Emmett Till was lynched. Much of this code is now illegal, and most Americans now also think that it is wrong. Yet, in the words of Glenn Loury, white Americans still think of black Americans as "them" rather than included in "all of us."[16]

A common survey reveals that most Americans distinguish between black and white. Researchers who study housing integration commonly ask whites and blacks whether they would move into a neighborhood with different proportions of the other race.[17] Most whites now say that they would move into neighborhoods with some blacks, but not a black majority. Many view such answers as progress, in that white Americans will now accept some black neighbors. But of course there is only one answer that would show no discrimination—100 percent. These attitudes perpetuate a distinction between "us" and "them." The experiments on group formation discussed in Chapter 4 show that it is remarkably easy to get experimental subjects to divide themselves into groups and treat other groups differently. They also form negative opinions about those assigned to a different group. Of course, these experiments pale in comparison to the race dynamics of American society. The real-world psychological effects on those who are treated as an out-group must be much more powerful. "They" are likely to adopt a view of themselves in opposition to the "us" of the dominant group. This rejection, of course, is self-affirming. In our language, it yields benefits in identity utility. We consider here the trade-offs between such benefits and the economic costs.

Does such an oppositional identity exist? Popular culture is full of expressions of opposition and difference, and there are debates about rap music and the message it sends to African-American youth. The expressions and consequences of such responses to racism occupy much research and writing on African Americans, as seen in the work of a long list of scholars, including Elijah Anderson, James Baldwin, Kenneth Clark, W. E. B. Du Bois, Michael Dyson, Franklin Frazier, Ulf Hannerz, bell hooks, John Ogbu, Lee Rainwater, and William Julius Wilson.[18]

The possibility of opposition is not just about African Americans. American history, as now told, has been rife with ethnic conflict: blacks in opposition to whites, Native Americans and Asian Americans in opposition to Europeans, Hispanics in opposition to gringos, and, of course, Europeans in opposition to other Europeans. A century ago, differences between Catholics and Protestants were as prominent as today's differences between whites and people of color. In the early twentieth century the "lace-curtain" Irish who tried to fit into the dominant culture were contrasted to their fellow Irish who rejected it.[19] William Whyte's *Street Corner Society* shows how such concerns played out minute by minute among Italians of Boston's North End at the end of the Great Depression.[20]

Nor is oppositional identity peculiarly American. Our chapter on schooling describes Paul Willis's work on class antagonism in an English school between the accepting, obedient "ear'oles" and the rebellious, disobedient "lads," who never missed a chance to disrupt the school day.[21] In the study of colonialism, Edward Said's *Orientalism* describes the formation of the Western stereotype of the "Oriental." He sees a major source of colonial power as coming from an ideal that only the colonizers can meet.[22] Such an ideal poses a problem for local educated and business elites. They may try to "pass," or to integrate with the dominant group, but they cannot be fully accepted. They are unable to fit the ideal to which they aspire, and instead, in their language, culture, and background, they are made to feel inadequate. The psychiatrist Frantz Fanon describes the effects on the personalities of colonial subjects, who wish to succeed economically but must also struggle to maintain their dignity.[23] Such ambivalence is a common theme in the autobiographies of colonial elites as well as of successful African Americans.

The autobiography of Jill Nelson, an African-American reporter, illustrates the difficulty of working within the dominant culture without betraying oneself. The following quote describes her reaction to a job interview at the *Washington Post:* "I've also been doing the standard Negro balancing act when it comes to dealing with white folks, which involves sufficiently blurring the edges of my being so that they don't feel intimidated, while simultaneously holding on to my integrity. There is a thin line between Uncle-Tomming and Mau-Mauing. To fall off that line can mean disaster. On one side lies employment and self-hatred; on the other, the equally dubious honor of unemployment with integrity."[24]

This dilemma is openly discussed. "When Keeping It Real Goes Right" in NiaOnline magazine gives tips from prominent black women executives on how to navigate a workplace "dominated by White men" and reassures its readers that "you don't have to sacrifice your identity as a Black woman in the workplace."[25]

An Identity Model of Poverty and Social Exclusion

Here we build a theory of identity, discrimination, and minority poverty. Again we follow the procedure from Chapter 3. We begin with a boilerplate model, and we add our three identity ingredients: social categories, norms and ideals, and utility gains and losses. In this model we pay particular attention to how one person's decision affects the utility of others. We see feedback effects that exacerbate the initial effects of discrimination. The more blacks who overcome the negative effects of discrimination and integrate, the more comfortable other blacks will be in making the same decision. But if initially enough blacks face rejection, then they will not try to integrate, and many will feel more comfortable remaining outsiders. Again, we emphasize that the root cause of this phenomenon is the dominant group's initial rejection of blacks. The social dynamics within the black community then aggravate the effects.[26]

The Procedure: Part 1. The boilerplate economic model here is similar to the boilerplate labor-market model in the previous chapter. There are now black and white workers (rather than male and female workers), and individual workers decide whether or not to work at a given wage.

The Procedure: Part 2. As before, we specify the social categories, the norms and ideals, and the losses in utility.

Social Categories. We posit two social categories, insiders and outsiders. White workers are all, by definition, insiders. Black workers can choose whether to integrate and join the dominant majority as insiders. Alternatively, they can be outsiders, who remain apart and adopt an identity in opposition to the insiders.

Norms and Ideals. For insiders, the norms dictate that they should work for the firms in this economy. In contrast, outsiders ("Mau-Maus," according to Nelson) feel that they should not be so submissive.[27]

Black workers then choose among three possibilities: to be an insider; to be an outsider who works; or to be an outsider who does not work. Each of these three options has its respective advantages and disadvantages, as they are associated with different levels of pay and self-respect. (In the language of the model, self-respect is identity utility.)

Gains and Losses in Identity Utility. The gains and losses in identity utility can be summarized as follows:

- A black who tries to be an insider will suffer from her lack of acceptance by whites. She is denied self-respect because she does not fit the insider racial ideal.
- An outsider who chooses not to work maintains her self-respect. But a black who wants to be an outsider but who, nonetheless, chooses to work for—or, more generally, to cooperate with—whites loses identity utility. She loses self-respect not because of rejection by whites (because she does not try to be an insider). Instead, she loses self-respect because her outsider ideal tells her she should not be working for (or cooperating with) whites.

- There are also externalities in this model. A black worker who chooses to be an insider loses utility when other black workers choose to be outsiders (and vice versa). This is because people often prefer it when their choices are confirmed by their peers.[28] They can also suffer from disapproval and ostracism if their peers have made different choices of identity.

Theory and Evidence

Again, it is no surprise that the conclusions of the model fit actual patterns. Standard economic models of discrimination against blacks, like those based on white managers' "distaste" for hiring black workers, predict that competition will eliminate discrimination. Although competition certainly has led to more black workers in the labor force and rising wages for some black workers, we also still see high levels of school dropout, crime, and drug abuse. From the point of view of an insider, such behavior is self-destructive. And standard economics, which presumes that people make choices to optimize economic outcomes, cannot explain it. But in an identity model, dropping out of school at an early age makes sense. It is rational when the alternative, which is working in the white world but not "making it," entails too great a loss.

The results in our model echo the findings of William Julius Wilson's *When Work Disappears*, which studies race, class, and employment in African-American inner cities. The model predicts that as wages fall, more black workers will choose to be outsiders. In the trade-off between work and dignity, dignity wins out, and more will choose an outsider identity. In addition, in our model, if blacks who choose insider identities move out of a neighborhood, more of those remaining become outsiders, and then yet more insiders will desert the neighborhood. They find it too uncomfortable to remain. Wilson argues that low wages and the exit of the black middle class are major reasons for poverty and dysfunction in urban African-American neighborhoods.

Potential Remedies

It is immensely useful to have a good theory of black/white disparities. Even if there remain many practical difficulties in its application, the theory gives a sense of the possible. It suggests, for example, that there are at least three ways to prevent black workers from dropping out of the labor force. The first is to eliminate the distinction between black and white in the insider ideal. Whites then no longer reject blacks. In this case, there is only one outcome in our model. All blacks simply choose to be insiders, so that the identity-caused disparities between black and white disappear.[29]

The second way is to change what it means to be black. Some readers may have already reflected that an oppositional identity, *per se,* does not imply self-destructive behavior. Rather, it is the norms associated with such an identity that may be self-destructive. Some African-American leaders, who have seen this problem with the norms, have been trying to change them. To "keep it real" does not necessarily have to mean dropping out of school or rejecting mainstream work norms. Many prominent black intellectuals, actors, and sports figures evangelize this second way. At the fiftieth anniversary celebration of *Brown v. Board of Education,* Bill Cosby gave his controversial "Pound Cake" speech: "[The civil rights activists] didn't do all that stuff so that [they] could hear somebody say 'I can't stand algebra' . . . and 'what you is.'"[30] Others, like Louis Farrakhan and the Muslim Program of the Nation of Islam, call for different types of change. Citing the experience of the last four hundred years, they demand a separate territory for African Americans.[31] They are the opposite of integrationists, but, like Cosby, they also wish to uplift the community. They want to end self-oppression with a change in values in favor of family, education, respect for women, and abstention from drugs and alcohol. This oppositional identity can entail working hard, staying in school, staying off drugs, and getting and staying married.

A third way is to limit the feedback effects. If we can break the chain whereby adoption of outsider identity leads others to choose it in turn, we will lower black poverty. We discuss below how public policies can change identity choices by cutting this feedback loop.

Policies: Affirmative Action and Job Programs

Many public policies have been designed to increase employment and to offset the harms of discrimination. In evaluating such programs, economists typically focus on conventional costs and benefits, such as gains in graduation and employment rates. Our analysis indicates that the impact of these policies may depend on their ability to influence the choice of identity, insider or outsider. Two examples, affirmative action and job training programs, illustrate.

Identity economics widens economists' evaluation of affirmative action. Most economic studies focus on the effect on those directly involved in a particular program.[32] Such a focus is too narrow. The rhetoric and symbolism of affirmative action affect social exclusion more generally. For example, California's Proposition 209, a ballot initiative that passed in 1997, effectively removed affirmative action in public universities as well as in government employment and contracting. These measures affect others besides potential college and graduate-school applicants. The measures and the debates surrounding them can affect minorities' general perceptions about whether there is a place for them in the dominant culture. In contrast, but also taking a general view, Glenn Loury has argued that affirmative action programs inherently portray blacks as victims, and thus, in our words, encourage outsider identity.[33]

Identity economics explains why job programs identical in terms of economic content but differing in structure may have very different outcomes. Consider the outcomes of two different U.S. government programs, Job Corps and Jobstart. Job Corps is a residential program that provides "at risk youth . . . classroom, practical, and work-based learning experiences [to prepare them] for stable, long-term, high-paying jobs."[34] The program has been successful in increasing earnings, but because it is residential, it is also expensive. To save money, the Labor Department started Jobstart, which was in all respects the same as Job Corps except that it was nonresidential. But Jobstart was not nearly as successful.

Our model can explain the difference. The trainees in the residential programs do not just learn the practical, marketable skills. Being isolated with others who were similarly motivated to learn, they also change their orientation. In terms of our model, the residential programs have the advantage of turning outsiders into insiders. The nonresidential programs, which were much less invasive of students' lives, had correspondingly less effect.[35] This interpretation is consistent with the argument that the residential programs teach social skills and new life habits, as these behaviors are also markers of an insider identity.[36] It is also consistent with findings in the chapter on schooling, where we saw that some schools, even in the worst neighborhoods, achieve remarkable success if they isolate their students and aggressively work to change their students' identities.

Conclusion

Beyond specific programs, identity economics can give us a general understanding of the nation's social and economic problems. The problems a nation solves, and the problems it lets fester, depend both on our understanding and on our will to resolve them. As we remark in the chapter on schooling, we see a need for much greater understanding and will in the United States to deal with the mediocrity of our educational system. Resources and a new economic approach are also needed to resolve continued social divisions.

Barack Obama has been a vigorous exponent of the idea that both whites and blacks need a deeper understanding of issues of race. His "A More Perfect Union" speech was a response to those who questioned his judgment in having Jeremiah Wright as his pastor. Wright was notorious for his sermons, for example, having pronounced shortly after 9/11 that "Americans' chickens are coming home to roost." Obama distanced himself from

Wright, but rather than disavow him altogether, Obama explained the reasons for black anger and also the reaction to it among whites.

> And occasionally [African-American anger] finds voice in the church on Sunday morning, in the pulpit and in the pews. The fact that so many people are surprised to hear that anger in some of Reverend Wright's sermons simply reminds us of the old truism that the most segregated hour in American life occurs on Sunday morning. That anger is not always productive; indeed, all too often it distracts attention from solving real problems; it keeps us from squarely facing our own complicity in our condition, and prevents the African-American community from forging the alliances it needs to bring about real change. But the anger is real; it is powerful; and to simply wish it away, to condemn it without understanding its roots, only serves to widen the chasm of misunderstanding that exists between the races.
>
> In fact, a similar anger exists within segments of the white community. Most working- and middle-class white Americans don't feel that they have been particularly privileged by their race. Their experience is the immigrant experience—as far as they're concerned, no one's handed them anything, they've built it from scratch. They've worked hard all their lives, many times only to see their jobs shipped overseas or their pension dumped after a lifetime of labor. They are anxious about their futures, and feel their dreams slipping away; in an era of stagnant wages and global competition, opportunity comes to be seen as a zero sum game, in which your dreams come at my expense. So when they are told to bus their children to a school across town; when they hear that an African American is getting an advantage in landing a good job or a spot in a good college because of an injustice that they themselves never committed; when they're told that their fears about crime in urban neighborhoods are somehow prejudiced, resentment builds over time.[37]

We see these disparate views on race and its consequences as resulting in a stalemate (the exact word Obama used), where the problems of the African-American underclass, as well as of all the poor regardless of race, have been left to fester. Rather than accept these problems as "ours" and work to solve them, people on both sides of the racial divide have become so angry that the commitment of resources necessary to overcome the racial differences is now politically impossible to muster. To use David Ellwood's phrase, we give "poor support."[38]

Our approach to this problem reflects the mainstream view in other social sciences; as we have seen, there is even one very prominent politician who understands and explains it in the same terms. Our method, the procedure from Chapter 3, brings identity, anger, and its consequences into a standard economic framework. Filling this gap in the economics of racial discrimination is only a small step in addressing black/white disparities. But perhaps ideas do have consequences. This new economics may just lead to new directions for how best to allocate scarce resources and how best to use them.

Part Four

Looking Ahead

NINE

Identity Economics and Economic Methodology

IN THIS BOOK WE modify and broaden economic analysis to include identity. The stick-figure *Homo economicus* that populated economic models beginning in the past century cared only about economic goods and services. Then Gary Becker (and followers) added all kinds of tastes to the utility function. This was followed by the addition of psychological aberrations from "rationality," especially cognitive biases. Identity economics is a next step in this evolution.

If identity is such a powerful concept, why has it taken us so long to get here? Why has not identity been part of economics before? This chapter offers some possible answers. In so doing, it self-reflexively studies our own theory. According to the standards of the economics profession, what is a good theory? What are the correct procedures for use of evidence?

Theory and Evidence

Economists have a remarkable consensus on how to conduct research. A good place to see the doctrine is Milton Friedman's essay "The Methodology of Positive Economics."[1] Of course, not every economist would agree with everything in that essay. But, at least broadly interpreted, Friedman has captured the basics of how economists think we should proceed: We first choose a model, or a theory. We then test the model against observations and reject it if it does not fit. There will also be back-and-forth between observations and theory, as each informs the other.

A good theory should, above all, meet the criterion of parsimony: Friedman tells us to "explain much by little."[2] By that criterion, in our view, identity economics is very parsimonious. Application of our simple procedure has shown that we can explain a large number of phenomena, including the nature of African-American poverty, the reasons why students drop out of school, the role of the Women's Movement, and why organizations work. This seems to explain much by little.

Even so, many would say our model is not parsimonious. Economists give precedence to older theories, which means that, according to standard practice, an economist should make the case for a new theory by rejecting the old theory. A theory must also generate falsifiable hypotheses. However, because of the difficulty of rejecting theories, which we describe next, this criterion gives currently accepted theories almost a free pass and renders almost all economic theories as unfalsifiable.

Friedman and most modern economists hold that statistical tests are considered the appropriate way to go about testing a model. But Friedman, writing in 1953, could hardly have anticipated the weak power of statistics in rejecting economic hypotheses. There are several reasons for that lack of power. The first is the advent of modern economic theory. At the time of Friedman's essay, an economic model typically assumed perfect competition. Uncertainty may have been mentioned, but it was an unusual feature. It might have been fairly easy to reject such a narrow theory on statistical grounds. But now, with the advent of game theory, accepted economics includes all kinds of strategic behavior; it also includes all kinds of asymmetric information; and with behavioral economics, it may even include psychological motivations, such as loss aversion and present bias. With this expansion of economic theory, a huge number of possibilities are considered more parsimonious by precedent than identity economics; and they must be exhausted before an economist should, by the norms of the profession, proceed to models where new factors play a role.

This proliferation of economic theory has brought economics much closer to reality, but it poses a nightmare for the logical-positivist economist. If she is lucky enough to reject one model, there is always another such model to take its place. And that is just the beginning of her troubles. Any statistical test of a theory requires specifying variables to a degree of precision considerably beyond that indicated by the theory. The economist almost always has wide choice over the specification of the independent variables (those on the left-hand side of the regression equations), the dependent variables (on the right-hand side), and many different aspects of functional form. If her estimation is across time, she must additionally estimate the leads and lags; she must choose the time period for her estimation (the beginning and ending dates) and also the periodicity of the data (should the intervals be weeks, months, years, or some other period?). If her estimation is across a population, she must decide whom to include and exclude. (For example, should she include just males, just females, or both? Should she include adults? If so, in what age ranges? Etc.) Thus, even in testing a well-specified economic model, the economist has many, many choices regarding how to run her test.[3] Because each of these decisions can be made independently, even the most straightforward test has literally millions of possible specifications. That makes it difficult to follow the dictum to accept the model unless it is rejected; it makes it difficult to falsify any theory. It is rare to find a model, no matter how silly, whose millions of specifications will be uniformly rejected.

Observation of the Small

Statistical tests in most empirical work have sufficiently low power that we should be looking for alternatives. Much of science comes from very careful observation of the small. This alternative method succeeds in many areas because the key to aggregate outcomes often lies in the microscopic. The most dramatic example of the relation between the small and the large is the structure of life itself. Francis Crick and James Watson conjectured correctly that if they could describe the crystalline structure of a single DNA molecule, they would have unlocked the code of life.[4] The duality between the structure of the DNA molecule and the way in which organisms are generated and reproduced is one of the most beautiful findings of science.

What are the implications of such an approach for economics? Standard economic methodology, with its emphasis on statistical analysis of populations, would suggest that intensive study of a single molecule would be an all-but-worthless "case study." Such observations are "anecdotal." In the case of DNA, the exact opposite is true. One rabbit looks much the same as another because of their common DNA; and differences among rabbits are due to the differences in their DNA. Codes are worth studying because, insofar as they are the same, they lead to duplication; insofar as they are different, they lead to differences. The ethnographies that we have studied aim to uncover the social codes of economic units, such as firms, schools, and households. It makes sense to study their social codes for the same reason it is worthwhile to study rabbit DNA: to understand both the similarities and the differences among them.

The internal consistency of these ethnographies gives a criterion for their validity, though a different one from a statistical test. Milton Friedman and others have warned us that we should be careful about drawing inferences from what people say: they may misunderstand their own motives, and they may be self-serving. But the best ethnographic studies have a check for this. From the many details they record, and the attention they give to the subtexts of what people say, they construct a consistent picture of people's behavior. Indeed, the very best ethnographic studies do not just record what people say; they decode what people say and do.

Causality

There is another, perhaps more direct, reason for studying the small. In most economic problems, causality could go two ways. For example, a change in price can result from a shift in demand or a shift in supply. One popular approach to identifying the cause is to look for "natural experiments," events where something outside the system causes only supply or only demand to shift. Our favorite example is the Mariel boatlift, which led to a large influx of Cuban immigrants into the United States in 1980. Fidel Castro's decision to allow a large number of Cubans to leave the country had nothing to do with U.S. labor-market conditions. The immigrants poured into south Florida, greatly increasing the local supply of low-skilled labor. The labor economist David Card then had a remarkable opportunity to study the effect of this influx on wages and unemployment.[5]

Despite the creativity of economists in hunting down such situations, and on occasion in generating experiments themselves, even the best of these studies leave us with questions. The studies that successfully identify causality are surely useful, but they may only hint at what we really want to know. For example, we earlier saw how Rivkin, Hanushek, and Kain showed, with a special data set, that teachers make a difference to students' academic performance. As important as that finding may be, it opens up another question: how and why do teachers matter? This issue is, of course, yet more difficult to explore with statistical methods. What is it that good teachers do—perhaps in their overall strategy and planning, or perhaps in their minute-by-minute interactions—that leads to their success?

To answer such questions, we need the type of information that can come only from detailed, careful observations. Such studies, like *The World We Created at Hamilton High, The Shopping Mall High School,* and *Learning to Labour,* give us windows into the lives of students. The parts of Coleman's *Adolescent Society* and Bishop and Bishop's study of school bullying that we have found

117

most useful have been their descriptions, not their (unavoidably weak) statistical tests.

Experiments

Laboratory experiments are another way to look at the small. Statistical tests using population data may have weak power; and extended fieldwork may not be feasible. But well-designed experiments can be a substitute. Just as experiments can test risk aversion, present bias, and strategic play, they can test identity economics. And indeed, as we discussed above, some experimental work already shows that identity and norms matter to economic outcomes.

The Problem of "Gentlemanly" Distance

Beyond passing empirical tests, most economists also believe that a good model yields surprising conclusions. A friend of ours has said that there must be a "gentlemanly distance" between assumptions and conclusions, otherwise the theory is vacuous. According to this view, the directness of our conclusions from our assumptions is a flaw. We are like the sage who explained movement by saying that it is due to the principles of locomotion.

We agree that conclusions should not be obvious. But there may be more than one way to reach nonobvious conclusions. The assumptions themselves may be new and thus may give rise to new insights. Take two propositions from this book:

- If tasks are tagged as male or female, men and women will work in different occupations, and women will have lower wages.
- If identity matters to workers, they will require less incentive pay when they think of themselves as insiders to the organization.

Neither of these propositions follows from standard theory. What is new in each is the assumptions. We know that there is little distance between assumption and result.

Indeed, there is a great deal of science in which a shift of assumption is the key insight. Once that shift is made, the results are obvious. Here again the work of Crick and Watson is germane. Once they had characterized the DNA double helix, the basis for the genetic code did not even need to be stated. As they wrote: "It has not escaped our notice that the specific pairing we have postulated immediately suggests a possible copying mechanism for the genetic material."[6]

TEN

Conclusion, and Five Ways Identity Changes Economics

WE HAVE USED identity economics to study work, school, and home. We have speculated on why economists have not previously considered identity. Here we look ahead and discuss five separate reasons, with illustrative examples, why identity enriches economic analysis.

Individual Actions

Identity affects individual behavior directly. This impact is most apparent in things people do that yield no economic benefit—often in activities that are costly, uncomfortable, and even injurious. Identity economics allows economists a simple representation of what could be labeled, literally, as self-destructive behavior, and actions that seem to make little economic sense.

Body Art and "Bad Choices." One of the most obvious examples is how people change their bodies to fit an ideal. An exhibit of the American Museum of Natural History was titled "Body Art:

Marks of Identity." The exhibit showed how, in past times, people bound the soft bones of children's skulls and feet; how they stretched their necks with rings; how they removed ribs to minimize waists; and how they shaped heads, even in Europe through the nineteenth century.[1]

According to Gerry Mackie, in early nineteenth-century China, some 50 to 80 percent of Chinese parents bound their daughters' feet. They did so largely because it was a requirement for a suitable marriage. But they also did it to conform to an ideal of how women should be. Footbinding was considered a mark of modesty, which made women more fertile and also more sexually pleasing.[2]

Body art is alive and well in the modern world, although with different ideals. Cosmetic surgery in the United States is a $13 billion industry.[3] But it is just one of many body-altering practices such as tattooing, body piercing (of the ear, nose, and navel, for instance), weightlifting, steroid use, circumcision, and dieting.

Identity economics not only helps us understand these wonts; it helps us explain "bad choices" more generally. The teachers in the school Paul Willis studied thought the lads made bad choices. But the lads themselves thought their "laffs" made sense. In general, people think others with different ideals make wrong decisions. That, of course, is our current-day perspective on the body art of past centuries: we wonder what moved those ancients to mutilate themselves as they did.

Charitable Contributions and Alumni Giving. Charitable giving is a rather different example of identity and norms driving individual actions.[4] Americans are great contributors to charities; overall donations exceeded $300 billion in 2008.[5] Identity economics can help us understand both the magnitude and direction of this giving. For example, donations to educational institutions alone amounted to $41 billion.[6] In the sometimes crazy world of standard economic theory, the University of North Carolina's development office could find it more profitable to solicit donations from a Duke graduate than from a graduate of UNC. Why? Because in the standard model, people would send their dollars to where their additional dollar would do the most good, and this could be the university with the lower endowment. Identity economics, by contrast, would predict correctly that, with rare exception, U.S. college graduates give to their own alma maters. Fight songs, football games, and other college rituals all reinforce their attachment to the institution, helped along by the development office. The song "Bright College Years" tells Yalies their charge: "For God, for country, and for Yale."[7]

Externalities

People's actions often affect others' well-being. Economists and policy makers make a great deal of what we call *externalities*. Let's go back to the example of the factory that emits too much smoke. Its owners do not suffer the costs experienced by those downwind, so there is a mismatch between private and public costs. Policies—like imposing taxes on emissions—can correct the mismatch. For similar reasons, we should be interested in externalities that result from identity utility. Externalities can be both negative and positive. The women who worked at Eveleth Mines were mistreated by their resentful male co-workers. But, as we see in experiments and on the shop floor, in-group identification can also lead to cooperation.

Insults, Hate Crimes, and Violence. Since the time of Gary Becker, economists have applied utility theory to crime and punishment. Identity economics significantly expands this theory by bringing in the effects of insult and injury. Perceived or real insults can be the source of much violence, as well as of escalating racial and ethnic strife. Once again, let us look at the detailed example. Men in the United States, into the nineteenth century, countered insults with a challenge to duel. Richard Nisbett and Dov Cohen at the University of Michigan uncover remnants of this practice in *Culture of Honor: The Psychology of Violence in the South*.[8] In an experiment, male students were asked to come to an office at the end of a narrow hallway. Along the corridor, an accomplice of the researchers bumped the student. Rather than apologize, the accomplice called the student an "asshole." The experimenters then measured reactions to this treatment. Stu-

123

dents from the South were more likely than those from the North—and also more likely than controls from the South—to fill in subsequent word-completion tests with aggressive words (for example, *g-un* rather than *f-un*). They also had higher cortisol levels. Insulted Southerners also revealed that the insult affected their self-image: in answers to survey questions, they were more likely to fear that the experimenter had a low opinion of their masculinity.

Such reactions to insult, as well as hate crimes, fit easily into our framework, and thus identity economics gives us a powerful instrument for studying crime, violence, and policies to counter them. Many public policies affect the incidence of such externalities and the costs of retribution. Bans on duels—first in the North, later in the South—ultimately put an end to the practice. Antilynching laws raised the penalty for maintaining the boundary between black and white.[9] Hate-crime legislation serves a similar purpose.[10]

Free Riders. In-group norms, on the other hand, can solve one of the leading problems in economics: the "free-rider problem." Public goods—like parks, national security, and public education—are costly to provide. Economic theory tells us people will try to "free ride"—to let others do the work and pay the costs. But, of course, many public goods are provided voluntarily. People vote to pay taxes to educate other people's children and to maintain parks they will never visit. Identity economics gives us a framework to study why and when they do so. Elinor Ostrom finds the solution to the free-rider problem in communities where people believe in norms for cooperation.[11] In public-good experiments, as we have discussed, people cooperate more with members of their own group. And empirical research in the United States shows that people in more ethnically homogeneous communities make larger contributions to education and other local public goods than those in more diverse communities.[12]

Creating Categories and Norms

Here we have often taken the social categories, norms, and ideals of a situation as given. But many people and organizations manipulate categories, norms, and ideals for their own advantage.[13] In our models, firms and schools that spend money to turn outsiders into insiders are doing just that.

Advertising. Advertising is the most obvious example of such manipulation. Its goal, of course, is to induce people to buy more of the advertised product. Not only do advertisers appeal to existing norms, but they also try to create new ideals. Marketing researchers and others outside economics have long understood this point.[14] Gender ideals and norms are again an obvious place to look, as in the Virginia Slims ad campaign discussed in Chapter 3.[15] Such ads do not fit a standard economic view of advertising, where advertising informs consumers directly about the existence or attributes of a product or signals the product's quality.[16] As the Virginia Slims ads illustrate, the purpose of advertising is often to make people want a product in order to live up to an ideal.

Politics. Politics, too, is often a battle over identity.[17] Rather than take voters' preferences as given, political leaders and activists often try to change identity or norms.[18] Some of the most dramatic examples of regime change involve changes in norms regarding who is an insider and who is an outsider. Fascist and populist leaders foster racial and ethnic divisions.[19] Symbolic acts and transformed identities spur revolutions. Mohandas Gandhi's Salt March sparked the Indian independence movement and a new national identity. The French Revolution changed subjects into *citizens*. The Russian Revolution turned them into *comrades*.

Identity is not a factor only in revolutions and large-scale regime shifts; it also plays a role in democratic elections. In the standard rational-actor model of electoral politics, people vote for the party or politician whose policies best promote their economic interests. In an extended model with identity economics, a voter would have not only economic interests but also an identity and norms and ideals, and incorporating these into the model would lead to quite different predictions. In practice, a great deal of politics involves such activities as the kissing of babies, the parading of flags, and positioning on social issues. Candidates who appeal to voters' ideals and norms may be elected even if their policies are contrary to voters' economic interests. This issue becomes yet more salient when marketing (as in the example of advertising) can place candidates closer to constituents' ideals or change their norms.

Identity and Regret

People often make decisions that come back to haunt them. We overeat, we smoke, we spend too much, and we regret it.[20] Identity economics greatly expands the study of such "time inconsistency." People have different selves at different points in their lives.[21] The new self could regret the decisions made by the old self. The preferences of the new selves come from the new identities and their associated norms and ideals. Sometimes these transitions are anticipated, and people plan accordingly. But often, people only imperfectly anticipate who they will later become. The norms and ideals can conflict, and people may regret past behavior. Some examples, classified by the frequency with which they occur, give us an appreciation for the range of such identity changes over a lifetime.

- *Lowest frequency.* Some types of identity are permanent. For example, race and gender only rarely change over the course of a lifetime.
- *Low frequency.* Some types of change in identity occur infrequently, on the order of once or twice in a lifetime. They are often marked by rites of passage, such as a baptism, a confirmation, a bar or bat mitzvah, a wedding, or a retirement party. Rites of passage mark social boundaries and are a classic topic of study in anthropology.[22] They move a person into her new situation and mark her transition for others in the community.
- *High and regular frequency.* Some changes occur at very high frequency, such as the daily transition between home and work. The imperatives of the workplace recede at home, as the imperatives of home recede at the workplace.

Choice of Identity

Economics is sometimes called the science of choice. The previous four sections discuss the influence of identity on choices of actions. But as we discussed earlier, identity itself can be a choice. To a degree, people can choose who they want to be. Here we briefly present three examples of identity choice, each of which has great impact on our economy.

Housewives and Motherhood. A clear example is the choice that a middle-class woman faces between pursuing a career and becoming a stay-at-home mom. In the past, norms gave college-educated women no such choice. In 1963, Betty Friedan's *Feminine Mystique* pictured the ideal of the suburban housewife: "Kissing [her] husband goodbye in front of the picture window, depositing [her] stationwagonsful of children at school, and smiling as [she] ran the new electric waxer over the spotless kitchen floor."[23] The transformation in women's roles from then to now can even be picked up in the statistics, as found by Claudia Goldin. In the 1970s, few teenage women expected to be employed at age thirty-five; now almost all of them do. Almost all college-educated women used to take on their husbands' names; now a significant minority retain their surnames. Women with high-earning husbands were much less likely to hold a job; now there is little relation between husbands' incomes and wives' employment. When wages fell, women dropped out of the labor force; now women are much more likely to continue working. Goldin concludes, "They have added 'identity' to their decision about whether to work."[24]

School Choice. We have already studied high school education and the choice to exert effort on schoolwork and graduate. But there is another basic choice: which school to attend. Parents often choose their children's schools. Slightly more than 10 percent of American students in grades K–12 currently attend private schools.[25] But that statistic understates, perhaps by a multiple, the role of private schools. During their school career, a much larger fraction of students (no one yet has calculated how much larger) will spend some time in a private school. These numbers suggest considerable disavowal of the public schools, because the financial sacrifices for even one year of private school are considerable: median private school tuition is as much as 5 percent of median family income. A breakdown of private school students shows that the bulk of such education is sectarian. Approximately 45 percent attend Catholic schools, 38 percent other religious schools, and 17 percent independent schools.[26] The choices between public and private, sectarian and nonsectarian schools are among many schooling choices. And school choice, along with the establishment of charter schools and the provision of tuition vouchers, is at the forefront of the education policy debate. Much of the discourse is about educational quality. But, as we discussed in our education chapter, identity economics suggests that identity and quality are intertwined.

Immigration. Immigrants often face a difficult decision. They must decide the extent to which they will integrate into their new country and whether to change their citizenship. Whichever choice they make, there are economic costs and benefits, and disapproval from those who have taken the opposite route. Again let us look at the small. Richard Rodriguez, a Mexican American who chose to be fluent in English at the expense of Spanish, describes the reactions of relatives and other community members. A trip to the store with his mother left a lasting impression: "*Pocho!* the lady in the Mexican food store muttered, shaking her head. I looked up to the counter where red and green peppers were strung like Christmas tree lights and saw the frowning face of a stranger. My mother laughed somewhere behind me. (She said that her children did not want to 'practice' their Spanish after they had started going to school.) My mother's smiling voice made me suspect that the lady who faced me was not really angry at me. But searching her face, I couldn't find the hint of a smile."[27]

Current political debates about immigration and language involve such conflict over norms and ideals. Once again, a new lens helps us understand the debate and the impact of policy.

Conclusion

This book is a primer on identity economics. Our aim has been to introduce identity in the simplest way. After developing our procedure in Chapter 3, we have seen it at work in example after example.

We are optimistic about the future of identity economics, for a number of reasons. The typical primer opens up a new world. For the first grader who reads for the first time, there are vast libraries yet to be read and yet to be understood. This primer should open a world to be studied. We attest to our own experience. When we began some fourteen years ago, we did not even have the beginning of a framework. We could not have systematically described, for example, Erving Goffman's visit to the merry-go-round and James Coleman's questionnaires in *Adolescent Society*, which asked students, "If you could be remembered here at school for one of the three things below, which one would you want to be: brilliant student, athletic star, or most popular?"[28] Goffman was looking for examples of *presentation of self*. Coleman was looking for students' *ideals*. Now our framework allows us to see the common principle underlying both: identity. This book reports on the results.

In the approximately ten years since we published our first article on the topic, "Economics and Identity," our economics colleagues have taken identity economics in directions that we never anticipated. They have applied it in the laboratory; they have given theoretical explanations for its origins; and they have even done some statistical analysis. Some of this work is described in this book.

We have every reason, then, to believe that this is just the beginning. Many standard psychological and sociological concepts fit our framework, with considerable generality and a common theme: self-image, self-realization, situation, in-group versus out-group identification, self versus other, social structure, power, and difference. In each of the five sections above, there are economic questions ripe for an identity approach. And we have not even touched on fundamentals such as the history of economic institutions, economic development, and the nature and boundaries of firms.

There are also deeper questions. Where do norms and identity come from? How do they change and evolve? What is the feedback between identity, economic policy, and institutions? What explains different identities and norms across countries? What might explain the rise and fall of group conflict? Asking these questions—and answering them—will have consequences.

Acknowledgments

WE BEGAN THE work described in this book in 1995, and many people and institutions have helped us along the way. Here we express our debt and gratitude.

First, we thank our editors. The original article "Economics and Identity" was published in the *Quarterly Journal of Economics* and was edited by Edward Glaeser and Lawrence Katz. Their comments were invaluable to sharpening our arguments, and their advice to apply our framework to numerous examples has guided us throughout this research program. John McMillan did us great service at the *Journal of Economic Literature*, where he pared down, tightened, and considerably amended our original manuscript of "Identity and Schooling." Andrei Shleifer, Michael Waldman, and Timothy Taylor helped us reformulate "Identity and the Economics of Organizations" for the *Journal of Economic Perspectives*. Shleifer alerted us to Lipsky's *Absolutely American*. And we are immensely grateful to Peter Dougherty at Princeton University Press, whose encouragement over many years, and whose continual advice and editing, has resulted in a manuscript that is much more focused and readable than our original efforts, as this book has grown considerably beyond the original journal articles on which it is based. We are also extremely grateful to anonymous referees for the *Quarterly Journal of Economics,* the *Journal of Economic Literature,* and the *Journal of Economic Perspectives,* and especially to three anonymous referees for Princeton University Press.

Many research assistants have helped us along the way, and we thank them for their uniformly good work and for their patience with us. They include Michael Ash, Paul Chen, Jennifer Eichberger, Cyd Fremmer, Alexander Groves, Joshua Hausman, Nisha Malhotra, Tomas Rau, and Eric Verhoogen. Their detailed comments on articles and previous versions of the manuscript have also proved invaluable and greatly bolstered our writings.

Many friends and colleagues have listened to us over the years and read our work as our thoughts about identity economics have unfolded. They have listened even in preliminary stages, and their many comments have strengthened our thinking. We are especially grateful to Claudia Goldin and Lawrence Katz as the first readers of "Economics and Identity" back in 1996. We thank everyone who gave us comments and challenged us as well as offering encouragement and support: Daron Acemoglu, Philippe Aghion, Siwan Anderson, Abhijit Banerjee, Kaushik Basu, Paul Beaudry, Gary Becker, Roland Bénabou, Timothy Besley, John Bishop, Barry Bosworth, Samuel Bowles, Robert Boyd, Gary Burtless, Jeffrey Butler, David Card, Alessandra Casella, Penny Codding, Stefano DellaVigna, William Dickens, Rafael Di Tella, Curtis Eaton, Catherine Eckel, Stuart Elliott, Ernst Fehr, Gary Fields, Patrick Francois, Nicole Fortin, Pierre Fortin, James Foster, Roland Fryer, Robert Gibbons, Herbert Gintis, Paola Giuliano, Lorenz Goette, Avner Greif, Richard Harris, Victoria Hattam, John Helliwell, Elhanan Helpman, Chaviva Hosek, Peter Howett, David Huffman, Aurora Jackson, Shachar Kariv, Botond Koszegi, Michael Kremer, David Laibson, Kevin Lang, Edward Lazear, George Loewenstein, Glenn Loury, George Mailath, Ulrike Malmendier, Eric Maskin, Robert Merton, Pascal Michaillat, Edward Miguel, Deborah Minehart, Joel

Mokyr, John Morgan, Andrew Newman, Philip Oreopoulos, Robert Oxoby, Janet Pack, George Perry, Shelley Phipps, Matthew Rabin, Antonio Rangel, Craig Riddell, Joanne Roberts, Francisco Rodriguez, Christina Romer, David Romer, Paul Romer, Seth Sanders, Kathryn Shaw, Robert Shiller, Dennis Snower, Anand Swamy, Richard Thaler, Eric Wanner, Kent Weaver, Robin Wells, Wei-Kang Wong, and Peyton Young.

Several people have read various versions of our manuscript and have made detailed comments, above and beyond the call of duty. They include Alex Haslam, Marion Fourcade, Irene Bloemraad, and Robert Merton. We are especially grateful for their guidance, which has greatly shaped our thinking and our writing. They changed the focus of the book and also honed our discussions of sociology and psychology.

We are grateful to the participants at the many seminars and conferences where we have presented our articles and this book. We thank the following institutions for inviting one or the other of us to discuss our work: Boston University, the Brookings Institution, Cornell University, Furman University, George Mason University, Georgetown University, Harvard University, the Institute for Advanced Study, James Madison University, Keio University, the London School of Economics, Massachusetts Institute of Technology, Northwestern University, the Ohio State University, the Russell Sage Foundation, Scranton University, Smith College, Stanford University, Tufts University, the University of Akron, the University of Antwerp, the University of British Columbia, the University of California at Berkeley, the University of California at Davis, the University of California at San Diego, the University of Chicago, University College London, Vanderbilt University, and Williams College.

Many institutions have helped us. Beyond our own universities —the University of California at Berkeley, the University of Maryland, and Duke University—we have been financially supported by the Canadian Institute for Advanced Research—George Akerlof in the programs on Institutions, Organizations and Growth and its precursors, and both of us in the program on Social Interactions, Identity, and Well-Being. George Akerlof has also been supported by the Brookings Institution and the National

Science Foundation under Research Grants SBR 97-09250 and SES 04-17871. Rachel Kranton was a visiting scholar at the Russell Sage Foundation and a member of the School of Social Science at the Institute for Advanced Study, and she also received the hospitality of the International Economics Section of Princeton University. To all of these institutions we are immensely grateful for their generous financial and logistical support.

Finally, we thank our families. Janet Yellen, George Akerlof's wife, has lived with, and supported, the cause of identity economics over many years. Robert Akerlof, who is an emerging scholar making his own mark in the field, has given us detailed running comments ever since he was a teenager in the 1990s. We are very grateful for his advice on our model in the section on organizations, and, even more important, for his judgment and comments as we brought our ideas together in this book. Rachel Kranton thanks her parents, Jack and Esther Kranton, who have given unfailing support throughout this endeavor. Her children, Lena and Sarah, have been the most joyful possible companions over the past eight years. We especially thank her husband, Abdeslam Maghraoui, whose own research and views on identity influenced our perspective and led us to question its role in economics. His book on political identity and democracy in Egypt, *Liberalism without Democracy: Nationhood and Citizenship in Egypt, 1922–1936,* was published just two years ago. We tremendously value his insights, his advice, and his support throughout. We are proud to dedicate this book to Robert Akerlof and Abdeslam Maghraoui as a way of showing our love for them and our special thanks for their deep contributions to our thinking and for their generosity and guidance while writing this book.

Notes

Chapter One
Introduction

1. Hopkins (2005, pp. 359–60); *Price Waterhouse v. Hopkins,* 490 U.S. 228 (1989). The $25 million figure comes from the Supreme Court case.

2. The court opinion records, "Of the 662 partners at the firm at that time, 7 were women. Of the 88 persons proposed for partnership that year, only 1—Hopkins—was a woman. Forty-seven of these candidates were admitted to the partnership, 21 were rejected, and 20—including Hopkins—were 'held' for reconsideration the following year." *Price Waterhouse v. Hopkins,* 490 U.S. 228 (1989).

3. *Price Waterhouse v. Hopkins,* 490 U.S. 228 (1989).

4. *Price Waterhouse v. Hopkins,* 490 U.S. 228 (1989).

5. Ellis (2008).

6. Goldman Sachs, "About Us."

7. Ellis (2008, p. 189).

8. Akerlof (1997). Titled "Social Distance and Social Decisions," this paper examined the consequences of social distance on social decisions, especially its effect on education and childbearing.

9. Our previous papers, Akerlof and Kranton (2000, 2002, 2005), are the basis for this book. George Akerlof has also applied the principles in those papers to macroeconomics: see Akerlof (2007).

10. *Price Waterhouse v. Hopkins,* 490 U.S. 228 (1989).

11. See Becker (1957, 1971, 1981); Becker and Lewis (1973).

12. Feminist economists have long argued for a wider vision of economics. See, for example, Ferber and Nelson (1993).

13. Donald Rumsfeld used this phrase in his tribute to Milton Friedman and said it also describes other valedictions at the celebration, including those from Gary Becker, Edwin Meese, and Alan Greenspan. For the text of the speech see Rumsfeld (2002). *Ideas Have Consequences* is also the title of a book by the University of Chicago philosopher Robert Weaver, published in 1948.

14. Keynes (1960, p. 383).

Chapter Two
Identity Economics

1. See, for example, Nash (1953); Varian (1974); Rabin (1993); Fehr and Schmidt (1999).

2. For a review of such results, see Camerer and Thaler (1995).

3. This interpretation of the work of Judith Harris (1998, 2006) comes from R. Akerlof (2009a, p. 4) and also earlier drafts.

4. Delpit (1995, p. 48). Students also understand ethnic social categories, and their behavior may reflect this awareness. In a survey of high school students in Miami and San Diego, Rumbaut (2000) found that grade-point average varied according to students' ethnic self-identification. (The analysis controlled for parents' socioeconomic status.) He also found that the more strongly students identified as American, the lower their academic achievement.

5. Goffman (1961, pp. 105–10).

Chapter Three
Identity and Norms in Utility

1. See, for example, Christakis and Fowler (2008).

2. Centers for Disease Control and Prevention (2002, Table 2).

3. See Waldron (1991, p. 993).

4. See, for example, Elkind (1985).

5. "You've Come a Long Way, Baby."

6. See Waldron (1991).

7. Fiore (1992).

8. U.S. Bureau of the Census (1992, Table 198, p. 128).

Postscript to Chapter Three
A Rosetta Stone

1. Sen (1997, p. 745).

2. See Friedman (1953).

3. See especially Bourdieu (2002).

Chapter Four
Where We Fit into Today's Economics

1. See Sherif et al. (1954).

2. Tajfel, Billig, Bundy, and Flament (1971).

3. See Haslam (2001).

4. Chen and Li (2009).

5. Other theoretical and experimental work explores a further departure from standard economic theory. It shows how pecuniary incentives can "crowd out" nonmonetary incentives, such as fairness, reciprocity, and adherence to social norms, thus leading to worse overall performance (Frey and Jegen [2001]; Rob and Zemsky [2001]; Huck, Kübler, and Weibull [2003]; Gneezy and Rustichini [2000]; Fehr and Gächter [2002]).

6. McLeish and Oxoby (2006). In an experiment that varies the salience of group membership, Charness, Rigotti, and Rustichini (2007) find that group membership makes a difference when it is salient but does not make a difference when it is minimal.

7. Ball, Eckel, Grossman, and Zame (2001); Butler (2008).

8. Steele and Aronson (1995).

9. Spencer, Steele, and Quinn (1999); Hess, Auman, Colcombe, and Rahhal (2003).

10. Hoff and Pandey (2004, p. 5).

11. Benjamin, Choi, and Strickland (2007) have also found in the laboratory that the priming of Asian-American identity affects the investment choices of Asian Americans; and the priming of racial identity of native-born African Americans affects their degree of risk aversion.

12. Glaeser, Laibson, Scheinkman, and Soutter (2000).

13. Fershtman and Gneezy (2001). The differential play was entirely a male phenomenon.

14. Goette, Huffman, and Meier (2006).

15. Gneezy, Niederle, and Rustichini (2003); Croson, Marks, and Snyder (2003).

16. Becker (1957).

17. Becker (1971, p. 1).

18. Becker (1971, p. 14).

19. Becker (1957, 1971).

20. See, for example, Becker (1968, 1981, 1993a, 1993b); Becker and Murphy (1988).

21. Becker (1996, pp. 3–23).

22. Stigler and Becker (1977).

23. Goffman (1959).

24. U.S. Military Academy at West Point, "About the Academy."

25. See Akerlof (1976) for such a treatment of norms.

26. For a discussion of such norms as social capital within closed communities, see Bowles and Gintis (2002).

27. Kandori (1992).

28. Young (2008). For a review article, see Burke and Young (2009).

29. Bernheim (1994).

30. Austen-Smith and Fryer (2005).

31. Amartya Sen has long emphasized the importance of norms and identity in his theoretical articles: see, for example, Sen (1977, 1985). His book *Identity and Violence* (Sen [2006]) shows how norms and identity can both foment and curb violence.

32. Elster (1989). Davis (2003) has also emphasized the importance of identity for understanding the role of the individual in economics.

33. Ostrom (1990).

34. Oxoby (2004). See also Kuran and Sandholm (2008).

35. Bénabou and Tirole (2006, 2007).

36. Horst, Kirman, and Teschel (2007).

37. Akerlof (2009a,b).

Chapter Five
Identity and the Economics of Organizations

1. See Lipsky (2003, pp. 145–54).

2. U.S. Military Academy at West Point, "U.S. Military Academy Mission."

3. The reviews by Prendergast (1999) and Gibbons (1998) indicate the pitfalls of monetary incentive schemes.

4. See Holmstrom (1982).

5. This point has been made by Lazear (1989). Also, workers' concerns with fairness introduce yet another reason why they will resist variation in monetary compensation (Akerlof and Yellen, 1990).

6. See Jacob and Levitt (2003).

7. Gibbons (1998) argues that subjective performance criteria and repeated interaction could improve outcomes. But these possibilities also entail new difficulties—for example, employees have the incentive to use productive time to influence their supervisors' evaluations, and new circumstances can lead firms to renege on long-term implicit promises to workers.

8. The classic works of sociology by Barnard (1938) and Selznick (1957) discuss such motivation. For example, Selznick describes the leader's responsibility as defining "the mission of the enterprise. . . . Truly accepted values must infuse the organization" (p. 26). Kogut and Zander (1996), who are modern expositors in this tradition, describe the role of identity for worker motivation.

9. See Besley and Ghatak (2005); Prendergast (2003).

10. Bowles, Gintis, and Osborne (2001) model the value of workers with "incentive enhancing preferences." Lindbeck, Nyberg, and Weibull (2003) find in the context of welfare and benefits programs that if the work norm is weak, then voters will choose less generous benefits. In this sense, countries with strong norms are countries that "work well." Their earlier paper (Lindbeck, Nyberg, and Weibull [1999]) showed that political equilibria may be characterized either by strict norms, few beneficiaries, and high benefits, or by loose norms, many beneficiaries, and low benefits.

11. Detailed versions of the model appear in Akerlof and Kranton (2005, 2008).

12. This outcome follows directly from the difference in costs of effort for different workers. The result, as such, is nothing new. What is new is the source of the cost difference—here it is whether or not the worker identifies with the firm.

13. But this is not a general result. In a model with more than two effort levels, if identity reduces the employee's effort costs, the firm may find it optimal to elicit yet higher effort. In this case, we could well imagine that when a worker is an insider, the firm would increase rather than decrease the variation in compensation used to motivate the employee. In this sense, monetary incentives and motivation by identity can be complements, rather than substitutes.

14. For a classic account of the nature of battle, see Keegan (1976).

15. There are many nonmonetary ways to induce identities that conform to the wishes of the organization. In addition to Haslam's (2001) comprehensive review of social identity theory, there are numerous reviews of the psychology of persuasion, including those by Aronson (1984), Brown (1990), and Aronson, Wilson, and Akert (2002). All of the biases described by Mullainathan and Shleifer (2005) in the interpretation of news are also of use to organizations in changing the self-perception of their employees.

16. See Janowitz (1960, pp. 61–62) and Rostker et al. (1992).

17. See Asch and Warner (2001). The paucity of monetary incentives is seen not only within the military but also in the comparison between military and civilian pay. For example, a 1955 comparison between U.S. Air Force brigadier generals and civilian executives of seemingly comparable position showed that the civilians had 60 percent fewer supervisees and charge over 94 percent less inventory, yet they received five times the pay of their military counterparts (Janowitz, 1960, p. 184). However, Asch and Warner offer an explanation for the narrow range of military pay that is different from ours. They emphasize that because of the lack of lateral entry, the military has to recruit its managerial talent early in their careers and from the bottom of the hierarchy. This restriction results in relatively high entry-level pay in the military. In their model, the option value of talent also explains the "up or out" structure and the unusually high retirement pay for military employees.

18. Besley and Ghatak (2005). Frey (2007) has explored the economics of the use of medals and honors.

19. There is some dispute regarding the nature of and changes in the military ideal both for enlistees and for officers. For example, Huntington (1957) sees the officer corps, even after World War II, as imbued with the military values of duty, honor, and country, while Janowitz (1960) sees the military ideal as evolving toward the ideal of civilian organizations. Ricks (1997) claims that the military has become increasingly different from civilian society.

20. See Moskos, Williams, and Segal (2000, p. 1).

21. Benton (1999, pp. 2–3, 8). Here we also see the notion propounded by Samuel Huntington (1957) of the military as a profession. Lipsky (2003) describes the popularity of this idea among the West Point brass during his stay there.

22. See Bradley (1999, p. 14), and the essay by General Malham Wakin, "Service before Self."

23. See Janowitz (1960, p. 129).

24. For the full text, see Fogleman (1995, p. 5).

25. McNally (1991, p. 101).

26. See Stouffer et al. (1949b, p. 131).

27. Stouffer et al. (1949a, p. 412).

28. See Erikson (1966).

29. Benton (1999, p. 41).

30. Becker (1968).

31. To give another example, in efficiency wage models of the labor market, workers exert effort because they are afraid of being fired if they are caught shirking, not because they enjoy their work or feel an obligation to earn their pay (Shapiro and Stiglitz [1984]; Becker and Stigler [1974]). Similarly, in principal-agent models like the boilerplate model of Chapter 5, workers put in high effort rather than low effort only as a response to variations in pay.

32. Lipsky (2003).

33. As quoted in Hodson (2001, p. 29).

34. Covaleski et al. (1998, p. 313).

35. See Peters and Waterman (1982).

36. Rodgers (1969, p.100).

37. Pepper (2005, p. 127).

38. Bewley (1999, p. 2).

39. Terkel (1974, pp. xxxi–xxxv).

40. Smith (2001, p. 30).

41. Juravich (1985, pp. 135–36).

42. Newman (2000, pp. 96–99).

43. See Burawoy (1979) and Roy (1953).

44. Burawoy (1979, p. 51); Roy (1952, p. 430).

45. Burawoy (1979, Chapter 4, especially pp. 82 ff.); Roy (1953, pp. 511 ff.).

46. Burawoy (1979, p. 84, quoting Roy [1953, p. 511]).

47. Burawoy (1979, p. 88).

48. See Homans (1951).

49. Seashore (1954). Of course, the assignments could not have been totally random because similar jobs demand similar characteristics, and friends may seek to work together. The problems here are the usual ones concerning self-selection and the identification of peer effects on individual behavior (see Manski, 1993; Durlauf, 2002).

50. Seashore's study also provides evidence for differences in the strictness of supervisors, as workers gave differing responses when asked whether their foreman was closer to "the men" or to "management."

51. Milgrom and Roberts (1992, p. 393).

52. Fast and Berg (1975, p. 6); Gibbons and Waldman (1999, p. 2388).

53. See Fast and Berg (1975, p. 8).

54. See Moore and Galloway (1992, p. xiv).

55. See Stouffer et al. (1949b, p. 136).

56. Stamberg (2001).

57. Nine Japanese fishermen on the *Ehime Maru* were killed. It was eventually uncovered that a group of oil executives and their wives were on an excursion on the *Greeneville*. The *Ehime Maru* had been sighted seventy-one minutes prior to the accident, but the presence of the civilians crowded into the control room is believed to have resulted in failure to recheck the fishing boat's position; thus the collision. For details, see Israel (2001).

58. Stouffer et al. (1949a).

59. Stouffer et al. (1949a, Table 13, p. 409).

60. Piece rates have advantages other than simplicity, as Gibbons (1987, pp. 413–14) writes: "Workers are paid for the work they do, not the work they could have done, and this seems likely to solve problems associated with both hidden information (adverse selection) and hidden actions (moral hazard)."

61. Weber (1978 [1914], pp. 958–59).

62. Thus we have another case of multitasking. See Holmstrom and Milgrom (1991).

Chapter Six
Identity and the Economics of Education

1. Grant (1988).

2. Peer effects would not explain why the performance of both the original students and the newly bused students would decline. On the contrary, they would predict that the performance of the old students would decline while that of the newly bused students would rise. See Epple and Romano (1998).

3. A notable exception is the work of John Bishop and Michael Bishop (2007), which we discuss below.

4. Grant (1988, p. 241).

5. Grant (1988, p. 36).

6. Grant (1988, pp. 35, 38).

7. Hollingshead (1949); Coleman (1961).

8. Hollingshead (1949); Coleman (1961).

9. See Coleman (1961, pp. 42–43).

10. See Eckert (1989, pp. 50 ff.).
11. Bishop and Bishop (2007).
12. Harris (1998).
13. Eckert (1989, pp. 51, 53–54).
14. Willis (1977).
15. Foley (1990). On Mexican Americans, see also Valenzuela (1999). Fordham (1996) provides a study of African-American students.
16. Foley (2001, p. 36) translates *vatos* as "cool dudes."
17. Foley (1990, p. 58).
18. Foley (1990, pp. 139–40).
19. Everhart (1983); Willis (1977); Weiss (1990).
20. These guidelines were distributed to all students in a handbook outlining their rights. Grant (1988, p. 53).
21. Grant (1988, p. 54).
22. Powell, Farrar, and Cohen (1985).
23. See Goldin and Katz (1997). This debate is well documented in Krug (1964, 1972). Ravitch (1983, p. 46) excoriates progressive educators who champion nontraditional high school curricula, emphasizing life skills relating to health, vocation, and family and community life.
24. Indeed, the school has been dubbed the "miracle in East Harlem" (Fliegel [1993]).
25. Meier (1995, p. 30).
26. Meier (1995, p. 50).
27. CPESS offers another example of the ways a school's disciplinary procedures delineate the community. Students sent to the director's office for misconduct are led through the Five Habits of Mind to sort out the problem (Meier [1995, p. 50]). Such a method would be ineffectual if the students did not already identify with the school and its precepts.
28. Comer (1980, p. 76).
29. It appears that academic achievement also markedly improved, although there seems to be relatively little evaluation data. See Comer (1980, p. 74).
30. Comer (1988, p. 219).
31. Comer (1980, p. 118).
32. See Core Knowledge Foundation, "About Core Knowledge."
33. See Parker Core Knowledge School, "Dress Code."
34. In an article early in the history of Core Knowledge schools, Datnow, Borman, and Stringfield (2000) found that in Core Knowledge schools, reading and math scores improved somewhat and knowledge scores

increased considerably relative to comparable schools. The Core Knowledge Foundation website cites evidence of success. For example, test results for students in Core Knowledge schools in Colorado, where they are especially popular, are higher than for the state as a whole. See Core Knowledge Foundation, "Core Knowledge Research." But in this, as in other studies cited, there is likely to be considerable selection bias. Other than these sources, there appears to be little evidence regarding the relative success or failure of Core Knowledge schools.

35. See Bryk et al. (1993, p. 146).

36. Bryk et al. (1993, p. 141): "Teachers convey an intrusive interest in students' lives that extends beyond the classroom door into virtually every facet of school life. In some cases it extends even to students' homes and families."

37. Bryk et al. (1993, p. 141).

38. Altonji, Elder, and Taber (2003).

39. Altonji, Elder, and Taber (2003) correct for selection bias by using the bias in the observables to correct for the bias in unobservables.

40. See Altonji, Elder, and Taber (2003, Tables 1 and 2, last line).

41. Similar conclusions have been drawn by Evans and Schwab (1995). An interesting puzzle is that the difference in achievement scores between Catholic and public schools is much less pronounced (see Altonji, Elder, and Taber [2003]). Reasons could be that Catholic-school teachers have less reason than public-school teachers to teach to the test. And if at Catholic schools there is a much greater chance that a would-be dropout is in attendance on the day of the test, there is another reason for downward bias. Neal (1997) finds that Catholic schools are very advantageous to urban minorities, for whom the local public schools are often of especially low quality.

42. See Kaufman, Alt, and Chapman (2004, p. iii). They find that the status dropout rate, which is the fraction of 16- to 24-year-olds who are not in school and have not completed high school, was 7.3 percent for whites and 10.9 percent for non-Hispanic blacks in 2001.

43. The fraction of 25- to 29-year-olds with bachelor's degrees in 2002 was 29 percent for non-Hispanic whites and 17 percent for blacks. See U.S. Census Bureau, 2003.

44. See Jencks and Phillips (1998, Figure 1, p. 4).

45. More precisely, if the rate of return is lower, then African Americans will leave school earlier. Empirically, we see that the rate of return is actually higher for African Americans.

46. Delpit (1995, pp. 58–59).

47. A. Ferguson (2001).

48. A. Ferguson (2001, pp. 64–65).

49. Cook and Ludwig (1997).

50. Akerlof and Kranton (2002, Table 3, pp. 1194–95).

51. Akerlof and Kranton (2002, Table 4, p. 1196).

52. We think that our modeling can also explain other findings, such as Ronald Ferguson's observation (2001) that in suburban Shaker Heights, Ohio, African-American students spend more time on homework than whites but are less likely to complete assignments. It may also explain the finding by Fryer and Torelli (2005) that in segregated schools, as in white schools, students' popularity rises with their grade-point average (GPA), but in integrated schools, popularity begins to fall when GPA rises above 3.5. Fryer and Torelli suggest that this is evidence that in integrated schools, African-American students become unpopular by "acting white."

53. This follows work summarized by Hanushek (1986), including his own. Ferguson (1998) has also analyzed the reasons for the white/black test-score gap.

54. Rivkin, Hanushek, and Kain (2005, p. 450).

55. Peshkin (1986, p. 289).

56. Henig (1993, pp. 105–6).

Chapter Seven
Gender and Work

1. See Goldin (1990, Chapter 3) for historical measures of occupational segregation. For 1970–90 figures, see Blau, Simpson, and Anderson (1998), who use the U.S. Census Bureau three-digit classifications of occupations. Because of changes in these classifications, it is difficult to bring these figures up to date to include the 2000 census (personal communication with Francine Blau).

2. See Blau Weisskoff (1972); Strober and Arnold (1987).

3. See Milkman (1987); Honey (1984); Pierson (1986).

4. For studies of nurses and of marines, see Williams (1989).

5. See Pierce (1995, p. 134).

6. See Padavic (1991).

7. U.S. Court of Appeals for the Eighth Circuit (1997).

8. U.S. Court of Appeals for the Eighth Circuit (1997).

9. See MacKinnon (1979) and Pringle (1988).

10. See Davies (1982); Kanter (1977); Pierce (1995).

11. In contrast, only 56.9 percent of secondary school teachers are female.

12. See Fisher (1995) and Williams (1989). Source for figures on percentages of women in different occupations in 2007 come from U.S. Census Bureau and U.S. Bureau of Labor Statistics (2008, Table 11, "Employed Persons by Detailed Occupation, Sex, Race, and Hispanic or Latino Ethnicity"). "Secretaries" refers to the classification "secretaries and administrative assistants." "Nurses" refers to "licensed practical and licensed vocational nurses."

13. Bulow and Summers (1986) and Lazear and Rosen (1990) give other reasons for women's lower attachment to the labor force; both offer some explanation for occupational segregation.

14. See, for example, Mincer and Polachek (1974).

15. According to Bergmann (1974), male employers are averse to hiring women for particular jobs and may collude to keep women out of high-paying occupations, reserving the gains for other males. In our theory, occupational segregation occurs because of employees' desires to maintain their gender identity.

16. Goldin (2006). We view the publication of Betty Friedan's *Feminine Mystique* in 1963 and the founding of the National Organization for Women in 1966 as marking the beginnings of the modern Women's Movement.

17. In 1968, the figures were 7.1 years for men and 3.8 for women (U.S. Department of Labor [1968], Table A). In 1998, the figures were 3.8 years for men and 3.4 for women (U.S. Bureau of the Census 2000, Table 664). The figures for the two years are not strictly comparable: in 1968 the question asked for the time elapsed since the beginning of the current *job*, whereas in 1998 it asked for tenure with the current *employer*. Median male job tenure has also been considerably affected by shifts in the age distribution of the work force resulting from both demographic shifts and early retirement.

18. See Blau, Simpson, and Anderson (1998).

19. Source: Blau, Simpson, and Anderson (1998, Appendix A-1).

20. See Blau, Simpson, and Anderson (1998, Table 3 and Appendix A-1).

21. The increased use of computers is the most notable change in technology over this period, but they are used intensively in few of the occupations with major changes in mix.

22. 42 U.S.C. 2000e–2000e17 (1982), Sections 703(a)(1) and 703(a)(2).

23. See Becker (1971); Arrow (1972).

24. 442 F. 2d 385 (5th Cir. 1971), *cert. denied*, 404 U.S. 950 (1971). *Griggs v. Duke Power*, 401 U.S. 424 (1971), a race-discrimination case, is an important precedent outlawing the use of test results and other criteria correlated with race or gender as employment screens.

25. 442 F.2d 385 (5th Cir.) *cert. denied*, 404 U.S. 950 (1971).

26. Cited in MacKinnon (1979, p. 180).

27. *Price Waterhouse v. Hopkins*, 490 U.S. 228 (1989). Cited in Wurzburg and Klonoff (1997, p.182).

28. 580 F. Supp. 226 (E.D.N.Y. 1983), *aff'd*, 755 F. 2d 913 (2nd Cir. 1985). *Berkman* followed the expansive view in *McKinney v. Dole*, 765 F. 2d 1129 (D.C. Cir. 1985), that "any harassment or unequal treatment of an employee or group of employees that would not occur but for the sex of the employee or employees may, if sufficiently patterned or pervasive, comprise an illegal condition of employment under Title VII" (cited in Schultz [1998, p. 1733]).

29. See Schultz (1998, p. 1770).

30. Franke (1995).

31. As a result, Schultz (2003) argues, companies have tended to prohibit innocuous sexual behavior while permitting gender-based job discrimination. For example, some companies have prohibited co-workers from dating. Fears of sexual-harassment lawsuits have even prompted companies to adopt policies of informal gender segregation, although such policies directly violate the intent of Title VII.

32. For an early treatise on gender and the economics of the household, see Folbre (1994).

33. Lundberg and Pollak (1993).

34. Hochschild (1990, p. 38).

35. In our analysis, the unit of observation is a couple-year for the years 1983–92. Couples were included in a given year if they were married, neither member was retired, neither member was disabled, and the couple had positive work hours, positive earnings, and positive hours of housework. We also only included couples with complete data from both members on earnings, work hours, housework hours, and number of children. The final sample had slightly more than 29,000 couple-years of observations. We define a husband's share of housework, *hswk*, as his share of the total performed by the couple. Thus we capture the division of labor even in households that hire outside workers. We estimate the following Tobit equation: $hswk = a + \sum_{i=1,2,3} [b_{1i}h_i + b_{2i}h_i^2 + b_{3i}h_i^3 + b_{4i}h_i^4]$ + error, where h_i is the husband's share of outside hours worked if in group i. The summation ($i = 1,2,3$) runs over three types of household: with no children or youngest child over age 13, with youngest child age 0 to 5, and with youngest child age 6 to 13. Controls were included for ages of husband and wife relative to population average, log of total income, and total hours of housework. Results were robust to different specifications and estimators and substitution of share of earnings for share of hours worked. The equations and confidence intervals are available

on request. (Men's reports of housework shares matched almost exactly women's reports in Preston's [1997] study of 1,700 scientists.)

36. Hersch and Stratton (1994) use the PSID (the Panel Study for Income Dynamics) to study whether husbands' higher wage incomes account for their lower shares of housework. The estimation here, in contrast, evaluates the asymmetry in the relationship between husbands' share of income and their shares of housework, and wives' shares of income and housework.

37. See Tsuya, Bumpass, and Choe (2000).

38. See Tsuya, Bumpass, and Choe (2000, Table 5, p. 208).

39. Source: Greenstein (1996, p. 586, Table 1, p. 590).

Chapter Eight
Race and Minority Poverty

1. See U.S. Census Bureau, *Historical Poverty Tables,* Table 2.

2. More than half of African Americans had incomes greater than twice the poverty level. See U.S. Department of Labor, Bureau of Labor Statistics (2006, Table POV01).

3. Myrdal (1944).

4. In 2002 the proportion of out-of-wedlock births was 68.2 percent. See U.S. Bureau of the Census (2006, Table 82). In 2007, 58.5 percent of female-headed families, with no husband present and with children under 5, were in poverty. See U.S. Bureau of the Census (2008, Table POV03).

5. Kling (2006, p. 863). Kling's source is Bonczar (2003).

6. This conclusion is drawn from statistics calculated by Holzer, Offner, and Sorensen (2004, Figure 2, p. 4). They show that between 25 and 30 percent of the noninstitutionalized labor force in this age group with this level of education was either unemployed or out of the labor force in 2000. They also report that 12 percent of black male youth are incarcerated (p. 6). In contrast, for Hispanics, the nonemployment rate for the noninstitutionalized labor force was slightly greater than that for whites, both about 10 percent.

7. See Neal (2006, Table 6, p. 546).

8. See Coate and Loury (1993).

9. See Bertrand and Mullainathan (2003).

10. See Munnell, Tootell, Browne, and McEneaney (1996, p. 26).

11. See Ayres and Siegelman (1995, p. 311).

12. For an argument that the facts are not explained by the traditional theory, see Neal (2005, 2006).

13. The rate of out-of-wedlock births in 2005 was 69.9 percent for non-Hispanic African Americans, compared to 25.3 percent for white non-Hispanic women. See Martin et al. (2007).

14. Levitt and Venkatesh (2000, p. 771). The gang leaders did much better, and this outcome might explain these low earnings if the foot soldiers expect to rise in the gang hierarchy. But even the earnings of the gang leaders were not all that high—about $100,000 in 1995 dollars (p. 775), fairly close to the earnings reported for new MBAs.

15. See Neal (2005, p. 7).

16. See Loury (2002, pp. 82–83). And James Stewart has also long called on economists to bring racial identity into our studies (see Stewart [1997]). His appendix gives a model where individuals have utility for racial identity.

17. See, for example, Farley et al. (1993) and Schelling (1971).

18. See E. Anderson (1990); Baldwin (1963); Clark and Clark (1965); Du Bois (1965); Dyson (1996); Frazier (1957); Hannerz (1969); hooks (1990); Ogbu (1974); Rainwater (1970); Wilson (1987, 1996).

19. See, for example, Miller (1985).

20. Whyte (1943).

21. See Willis (1977).

22. Said (1978). Also see Bhabha (1983) and Fanon (1967).

23. Compare for example Gandhi (1966) and Fanon (1967), which describe the colonial experience, with Fulwood (1996), Staples (1994), and Rodriguez (1982), which represent the experience of African Americans and Hispanics in the United States.

24. See Nelson (1993, p. 10). The colonial origin of her term *Mau-Mau-ing* is suggestive of our claim of the similarity between the position of colonial subjects and African Americans.

25. NIAonline (2005).

26. Darity, Mason, and Stewart (2006) build an evolutionary model in which racial identity emerges as an equilibrium.

27. Elkins (2006) has described the Mau Mau rebellion in Kenya, where the British brutally imprisoned tens of thousands of Kikuyus. This response illustrates, once again, the differential treatment of "us" and "them."

28. See R. Akerlof (2009a) for a model where people want to have the same beliefs as their associates, which he calls desire for confirmation of belief.

29. For complete description of the model and the equilibrium outcomes, see Akerlof and Kranton (2003).

30. See "Dr. Bill Cosby Speaks" (2004).

31. See Nation of Islam, "What the Muslims Want."
32. See, for example, Dickens and Kane (1996).
33. See Loury (1995).
34. See U.S. Department of Labor, *Find It! By Topic.*
35. The Center for Employment and Training in San Jose was the one re-markable exception, a Jobstart program that showed a considerable increase in earnings. See Stanley, Katz, and Krueger (1998).
36. Heckman (1999).
37. "Text of Obama's Speech: A More Perfect Union" (2008).
38. Ellwood (1988).

Chapter Nine
Identity Economics and Economic Methodology

1. Friedman (1953, p. 3).
2. Friedman (1953, pp. 14, 10). Friedman calls for "simplicity." Today's economists use the word "parsimony."
3. Furthermore, the researcher should have less confidence in her spec-ification of the model than in the more general theoretical model. Hausman (1992) notes that this requirement can make economic the-ories de facto unfalsifiable. A model's failure of a statistical test is of-ten interpreted as a problem with the model's econometric specifica-tion, rather than with the theory itself.
4. As described by Watson (1969).
5. Card (1990).
6. Watson and Crick (1953, p. 737).

Chapter Ten
Conclusion, and Five Ways Identity Changes Economics

1. Paraphrased from the description of the exhibit at the American Mu-seum of Natural History, "Body Art: Marks of Identity."
2. See Mackie (1996, pp. 1001–2).
3. See American Society of Aesthetic Plastic Surgery (2008).
4. James Andreoni (1990) builds a general utility function in which in-dividuals have tastes for giving to charity: it gives them a "warm glow."
5. Giving USA Foundation (2008).
6. Giving USA Foundation (2008).
7. The last four lines of this song are: "Oh, let us strive that ever we / May let these words our watch-cry be, / Where'er upon life's sea we sail: / 'For God, for Country and for Yale!'"

8. Nisbett and Cohen (1996). For a description of this "culture of honor," see also Butterfield (1995). "Gentlemen" reacted to insult by engaging in duels. Lower-class men fought with hands and fists, with no holds barred.

9. For a study of the geographic distribution of lynching, see Tolnay, Deane, and Beck (1996).

10. All these laws seek to protect the minority from the majority, or the majority from itself. But they were not enacted without opposition. Thus, identity externalities are a new example of a classic problem of evaluating the impact of policy. Bans on gay marriage, antidiscrimination laws, and laws prescribing morality are all examples of the conflict of the Paretian liberal (see (Sen [1970]). It is not possible to protect one person against the externalities caused by another's choices and at the same time protect the first from the response of the second. There is a conflict between protecting the rights of individuals who engage in certain activities and suppressing these same activities because they cause others discomfort and anxiety.

11. Ostrom (1990).

12. Alesina, Baqir, and Easterly (1999); Miguel and Gugerty (2005).

13. Thus identity economics gives another way to understand endogenous preferences. See Bowles (1998).

14. Much advertising is targeted at particular social groups and appeals to societal norms and ideals. See de Grazia (1996) for historical studies of advertising and other influences on gender and consumption.

15. See also TobaccoDocuments.Org, "Tobacco Documents Online."

16. See Bagwell (2007).

17. For theory and analysis of politics and identity, see, for example, Anderson (1983), Norton (1988), and Connolly (1991).

18. Romer (1994) has considered the possibility that politicians can manipulate voters' emotions, in particular their "anger," and thereby affect political outcomes.

19. Glaeser (2005).

20. There is a long literature on the economics and psychology of time inconsistency. See, for example, Strotz (1956); Phelps and Pollak (1968); Thaler and Shefrin (1981); Loewenstein (1987); Loewenstein and Thaler (1989); Loewenstein and Prelec (1992); Ainslie (1992); Laibson (1997); Laibson, Repetto, and Tobacman (1998).

21. See, for example, Fudenberg and Levine (2006).

22. Turner (1995).

23. Friedan (1963, p. 18).

24. See Goldin (2006, p. 13).

25. In 2006, 5.1 million students were enrolled in private schools in grades K–12; 49.1 million were in public schools in grades K–12. U.S. Bureau of the Census (2009).

26. 2.25 million students were in Catholic schools; 1.89 million were in "other religious schools"; and 0.86 million were in nonsectarian schools. U.S. Bureau of the Census (2009, Table 254).

27. Rodriguez (1982, p. 29).

28. Coleman (1961, p. 28). This was the question for boys. For girls, "leader in activities" was substituted for "athletic star."

References

Ainslie, George. 1992. *Picoeconomics.* Cambridge: Cambridge University Press.

Akerlof, George A. 1976. "The Economics of Caste and of the Rat Race and Other Woeful Tales." *Quarterly Journal of Economics* 90 (4): 599–617.

———. 1997. "Social Distance and Social Decisions." *Econometrica* 65 (5): 1005–27.

———. 2007. "The Missing Motivation in Macroeconomics." *American Economic Review* 97 (1): 5–36.

Akerlof, George A., and Rachel E. Kranton. 2000. "Economics and Identity." *Quarterly Journal of Economics* 115 (3): 715–53.

———. 2002. "Identity and Schooling: Some Lessons for the Economics of Education." *Journal of Economic Literature* 40 (4): 1167–1201.

———. 2003. "A Model of Poverty and Oppositional Culture." In Kaushik Basu, Pulin Nayak, and Ranjan Ray, eds., *Markets and Governments.* New Delhi: Oxford University Press.

———. 2005. "Identity and the Economics of Organizations." *Journal of Economic Perspectives* 19 (1): 9–32.

———. 2008. "Identity, Supervision, and Work Groups." *American Economic Review* 98 (2): 212–17.

Akerlof, George A., and Janet L. Yellen. "The Fair Wage–Effort Hypothesis and Unemployment." *Quarterly Journal of Economics* 105 (2): 255–83.

Akerlof, Robert J. 2009a. "A Theory of Social Motivation." Chapter 1 in "Essays in Organizational Economics." PhD thesis, Harvard University, Cambridge, MA.

———. 2009b. "A Theory of Authority." Chapter 2 in "Essays in Organizational Economics." PhD thesis, Harvard University, Cambridge, MA.

Alesina, Alberto, Reza Baqir, and William Easterly. 1999. "Public Goods and Ethnic Divisions." *Quarterly Journal of Economics* 114 (4): 1243–84.

Altonji, Joseph G., Todd R. Elder, and Christopher R. Taber. 2003. "Selection on Observed and Unobserved Variables: Assessing the Effectiveness of Catholic Schools." Unpublished paper, Northwestern University.

American Museum of Natural History. n.d. "Body Art: Marks of Identity." www.amnh.org/exhibitions/bodyart/glossary.html.

American Society of Aesthetic Plastic Surgery. 2008. "Quick Facts: Highlights of the ASAPS 2007 Statistics on Cosmetic Surgery." www.surgery.org/sites/default/files/statsquickfacts.pdf.

Anderson, Benedict. 1983. *Imagined Communities.* New York: Verso, 1983.

Anderson, Elijah. 1990. *Streetwise: Race, Class, and Change in an Urban Community.* Chicago: University of Chicago Press.

Andreoni, James. 1990. "Impure Altruism and Donations to Public Goods: A Theory of Warm-Glow Giving." *Economic Journal* 100 (401): 464–77.

Aronson, Elliot D. 1984. *The Social Animal.* 4th ed. New York: Freeman.

Aronson, Elliot D., Timothy D. Wilson, and Robin M. Akert. 2002. *Social Psychology.* 4th ed. Englewood Cliffs, NJ: Prentice-Hall.

Arrow, Kenneth J. 1972. "Models of Job Discrimination," and appendix, "Some Mathematical Models of Race Discrimination in the Labor Market." In Anthony H. Pascal, ed., *Racial Discrimination in Economic Life.* Lexington, MA: Heath.

Asch, Beth J., and John T. Warner. 2001. "A Theory of Compensation and Personnel Policy in Hierarchical Organizations with Application to the United States Military." *Journal of Labor Economics* 19 (3): 523–62.

Austen-Smith, David, and Roland G. Fryer Jr. 2005. "An Economic Analysis of 'Acting White.'" *Quarterly Journal of Economics* 120 (2): 551–83.

Ayres, Ian, and Peter Siegelman. 1995. "Race and Gender Discrimination in Bargaining for a New Car." *American Economic Review* 85 (3): 304–21.

Bagwell, Kyle. 2007. "The Economic Analysis of Advertising." In Mark Armstrong and Rob Porter, eds., *Handbook of Industrial Organization.* Vol. 3. Amsterdam: North-Holland.

Baldwin, James. 1963. *The Fire Next Time.* New York: Dial Press.

Ball, Sheryl, Catherine Eckel, Philip J. Grossman, and William Zame. 2001. "Status in Markets." *Quarterly Journal of Economics* 116 (1): 161–88.

Barnard, Chester I. 1938. *The Functions of the Executive.* Cambridge, MA: Harvard University Press.

Becker, Gary S. 1957. *The Economics of Discrimination.* Chicago: University of Chicago Press.

———. 1968. "Crime and Punishment: An Economic Approach." *Journal of Political Economy* 76 (2): 169–217.

———. 1971. *The Economics of Discrimination.* 2nd ed. Chicago: University of Chicago Press.

———. 1981. "Altruism in the Family and Selfishness in the Market Place." *Economica* n.s. 48 (189): 1–15.

———. 1993a. "A Theory of Marriage: Part I." *Journal of Political Economy* 81 (4): 813–46.

———. 1993b. "A Theory of Marriage: Part II." *Journal of Political Economy* 82 (2), part 2, S11–S26.

———. 1996. *Accounting for Tastes.* Cambridge, MA: Harvard University Press.

Becker, Gary S., and H. Gregg Lewis. 1973. "On the Interaction between the Quantity and Quality of Children." *Journal of Political Economy* 81 (2), part 2, S279–S288.

Becker, Gary S., and Kevin M. Murphy. 1988. "A Theory of Rational Addiction." *Journal of Political Economy* 96 (4): 675–700.

Becker, Gary S., and George J. Stigler. 1974. "Law Enforcement, Malfeasance, and the Compensation of Enforcers." *Journal of Legal Studies* 3 (1): 1–18.

Bénabou, Roland, and Jean Tirole. 2006. "Incentives and Prosocial Behavior." *American Economic Review* 96 (5): 1652–78.

———. 2007. "Identity, Dignity and Taboos: Beliefs as Assets." Center for Economic Policy Research, CEPR Discussion Paper 6123.

Benjamin, Daniel J., James J. Choi, and A. Joshua Strickland. 2007. "Social Identity and Preferences." National Bureau of Economic Research Working Paper 13309. July.

Benton, Jeffrey C. 1999. *Air Force Officer's Guide.* 32nd ed. Mechanicsburg, PA: Stackpole Books.

Bergmann, Barbara R. 1974. "Occupational Segregation, Wages and Profits When Employers Discriminate by Race or Sex." *Eastern Economics Journal* 1 (2): 103–10.

Bernheim, Douglas. 1994. "A Theory of Conformity." *Journal of Political Economy* 102 (5): 841–77.

Bertrand, Marianne, and Sendhil Mullainathan. 2003. "Are Emily and Greg More Employable than Lakisha and Jamal? A Field Experiment on Labor Market Discrimination." National Bureau of Economic Research, Working Paper 9873. July.

Besley, Timothy, and Maitreesh Ghatak. 2005. "Competition and Incentives with Motivated Agents." *American Economic Review* 95 (3): 616–36.

Bewley, Truman F. 1999. *Why Wages Don't Fall during a Recession.* Cambridge, MA: Harvard University Press.

Bhabha, Homi. 1983. "Difference, Discrimination, and the Discourse of Colonialism." In F. Barker, ed. *The Politics of Theory.* London: Colchester.

Bishop, John H., and Michael M. Bishop. 2007. "An Economic Theory of Academic Engagement Norms: The Struggle for Popularity and Normative Hegemony in Secondary Schools." Ithaca, NY: Cornell University, School of Industrial and Labor Relations, Center for Advanced Human Resource Studies, Working Paper 07–14. September.

Blau, Francine D., Patricia Simpson, and Deborah Anderson. 1998. "Continuing Progress? Trends in Occupational Segregation in the United States over the 1970s and 1980s." National Bureau of Economic Research, Working Paper No. 6716. September.

Blau Weisskoff, Francine. 1972. "'Women's Place' in the Labor Market." *American Economic Review* 62 (2): 161–66.

Bonczar, Thomas P. 2003. *Prevalence of Imprisonment in the U. S. Population, 1974–2001* (NCJ *197976*). Washington, DC: U.S. Department of Justice, Bureau of Justice Statistics.

Bourdieu, Pierre. 2002. *Distinction: A Social Critique of the Judgement of Taste.* Trans. Richard Nice. Cambridge, MA: Harvard University Press.

Bowles, Samuel. 1998. "Endogenous Preferences: The Cultural Consequences of Markets and Other Economic Institutions." *Journal of Economic Literature* 36 (1): 75–111.

Bowles, Samuel, and Herbert Gintis. 2002. "'Social Capital and Community Governance." *Economic Journal* 112 (483): F419–F436.

Bowles, Samuel, Herbert Gintis, and Melissa Osborne. 2001. "The Determinants of Earnings: A Behavioral Approach." *Journal of Economic Literature* 39 (4): 1137–76.

Bradley, Omar N. 1999. *A Soldier's Story.* New York: Random House.

Brown, Roger. 1990. *Social Psychology: The Second Edition.* New York: Simon and Schuster.

Bryk, Anthony S., Valerie E. Lee, and Peter B. Holland. 1993. *Catholic Schools and the Common Good.* Cambridge, MA: Harvard University Press.

Bulow, Jeremy I., and Lawrence H. Summers. 1986. "A Theory of Dual Labor Markets with Application to Industrial Policy, Discrimination and Keynesian Unemployment." *Journal of Labor Economics* 4 (3), part 1, 376–415.

Burawoy, Michael. 1979. *Manufacturing Consent: Changes in the Labor Process under Monopoly Capitalism.* Chicago: University of Chicago Press.

Burke, Mary H., and H. Peyton Young. 2009. "Social Norms." In Alberto Bisin, Jess Benhabib, and Matthew Jackson, eds., *The Handbook of Social Economics.* Amsterdam: North-Holland.

Butler, Jeffrey. 2008. "Trust, Truth, Status, and Identity: An Experimental

Inquiry." Unpublished paper, Department of Economics, University of California at Berkeley, March.

Butterfield, Fox. 1995. *All God's Children: The Bosket Family and the American Tradition of Violence*. New York: Avon Books.

Camerer, Colin, and Richard H. Thaler. 1995. "Anomalies: Ultimatums, Dictators, and Manners." *Journal of Economic Perspectives* 9 (2): 209–19.

Card, David. 1990. "The Impact of the Mariel Boatlift on the Miami Labor Market." *Industrial and Labor Relations Review* 43 (2): 245–57.

Centers for Disease Control and Prevention. 2002. "Annual Smoking-Attributable Mortality, Years of Potential Life Lost, and Economic Costs —United States, 1995–1999." *Morbidity and Mortality Weekly Report*. April 12. www.cdc.gov/mmwr/preview/mmwrhtml/mm5114a2.htm.

Charness, Gary, Luca Rigotti, and Aldo Rustichini. 2007. "Individual Behavior and Group Membership." *American Economic Review* 97 (4): 1340–52.

Chen, Yan, and Sherry Xin Li. 2009. "Group Identity and Social Preferences." *American Economic Review* 99 (1): 431–57.

Christakis, Nicholas A., and James H. Fowler. 2008. "The Collective Dynamics of Smoking." *New England Journal of Medicine* 358 (21): 2249–58.

Clark, Kenneth B., and Mamie P. Clark. 1950. "Emotional Factors in Racial Identification and Preference in Negro Children." *Journal of Negro Education* 19 (3): 341–50.

Coate, Stephen, and Glenn C. Loury. 1993. "Will Affirmative-Action Policies Eliminate Negative Stereotypes?" *American Economic Review* 83 (5): 1220–40.

Coleman, James S. 1961. *The Adolescent Society: The Social Life of the Teenager and Its Impact on Education*. New York: Free Press.

Comer, James P. 1980. *School Power: Implications of an Intervention Project*. New York: Free Press.

———. 1988. *Maggie's American Dream: The Life and Times of a Black Family*. New York: New American Library.

Connolly. William. 1991. *Identity/Difference*. Ithaca, NY: Cornell University Press, 1991.

Cook, Philip J., and Jens Ludwig. 1997. "Weighing the Burden of 'Acting White': Are There Race Differences in Attitudes toward Education?" *Journal of Policy Analysis and Management* 16 (2): 256–78.

Core Knowledge Foundation. n.d. "About Core Knowledge." www.core knowledge.org/CKproto2/about/index.htm#BEN.

———. n.d. "Core Knowledge Research." http://coreknowledge.org/CK/about/research/eval12_2002.htm.

Covaleski, Mark A., Mark W. Dirsmith, James B. Heian, and Sajay Samuel. 1998. "The Calculated and the Avowed: Techniques of Discipline and Struggles over Identity in Big Six Public Accounting Firms." *Administrative Science Quarterly* 43 (2): 293–327.

Croson, Rachel T., Melanie B. Marks, and Jessica Snyder. 2003. "Groups Work for Women: Gender and Group Identity in the Provision of Public Goods." Unpublished paper, Wharton School, University of Pennsylvania. April.

Darity, William A., Jr., Patrick L. Mason, and James B. Stewart. 2006. "The Economics of Identity: the Origin and Persistence of Racial Identity Norms." *Journal of Economic Behavior and Organization* 60 (3): 283–305.

Datnow, Amanda, Geoffrey Borman, and Sam Stringfield. 2000. "School Reform through a Highly Specified Curriculum: Implementation and Effects of the Core Knowledge Sequence." *Elementary School Journal* 101 (2): 167–91.

Davies, Margery. 1982. *Women's Place Is at the Typewriter: Office Work and Office Workers, 1870–1930*. Philadelphia: Temple University Press.

Davis, John B. 2003. *The Theory of the Individual in Economics: Identity and Value.* London: Routledge.

de Grazia, Victoria. 1996. *The Sex of Things: Gender and Consumption in Historical Perspective.* Berkeley: University of California Press.

Delpit, Lisa. 1995. *Other People's Children: Cultural Conflict in the Classroom.* New York: New Press.

Dickens, William T., and Thomas J. Kane. 1996. *Racial and Ethnic Preference in College Admissions.* Brookings Institution, Brookings Policy Brief No. 9. November.

"Dr. Bill Cosby Speaks." 2004. www.eightcitiesmap.com/transcript_bc.htm.

Du Bois, William E. B. 1965. *The Souls of Black Folk.* Greenwich, CT: Fawcett Publications.

Durlauf, Steven N. 2002. "On the Empirics of Social Capital." *Economic Journal* 112 (483): 459–79.

Dyson, Michael E. 1996. *Between God and Gangsta Rap: Bearing Witness to Black Culture.* New York: Oxford University Press.

Eckert, Penelope. 1989. *Jocks and Burnouts: Social Categories and Identity in the High School.* New York: Teachers College Press.

Elkind, Andrea K. 1985. "The Social Definition of Women's Smoking Behavior." *Social Science and Medicine* 20 (12): 1269–78.

Elkins, Caroline. 2006. *Imperial Reckoning: The Untold Story of Britain's Gulag in Kenya.* New York: Henry Holt.

Ellis, Charles D. 2008. *The Partnership: The Making of Goldman Sachs.* New York: Penguin.

Ellwood, David T. 1988. *Poor Support: Poverty in the American Family.* New York: Basic Books.

Elster, Jon. 1989. *The Cement of Society: A Study of Social Order.* Cambridge: Cambridge University Press.

Epple, Dennis, and Richard E. Romano. 1998. "Competition between Private and Public Schools, Vouchers, and Peer Group Effects." *American Economic Review* 88 (1): 33–62.

Erikson, Kai. 1996. *The Wayward Puritans: A Study in the Sociology of Deviance.* New York: Wiley.

Evans, William N., and Robert M. Schwab. 1995. "Finishing High School and Starting College: Do Catholic Schools Make a Difference?" *Quarterly Journal of Economics* 110 (4): 941–74.

Everhart, Richard. 1983. *Reading, Writing, and Resistance: Adolescence and Labor in a Junior High School.* London: Routledge and Kegan Paul.

Fanon, Frantz. 1967. *Black Skin, White Masks.* New York: Grove Press.

Farley, Reynolds, Charlotte Steeh, Tara Jackson, Maria Krysan, and Keith Reeves. 1993. "Continued Racial Segregation in Detroit: 'Chocolate City, Vanilla Suburbs,' Revisited." *Journal of Housing Research* 4 (1): 1–38.

Fast, Norman, and Norman Berg. 1975. *The Lincoln Electric Company.* Harvard Business School Case Study 9–376–028. Boston, MA: Harvard Business School Publishing.

Fehr, Ernst, and Simon Gächter. 2002. "Do Incentive Contracts Undermine Voluntary Cooperation?" Institute for Empirical Research in Economics, University of Zürich, Working Paper No. 34. April.

Fehr, Ernst, and Klaus M. Schmidt. 1999. "A Theory of Fairness, Competition, and Cooperation." *Quarterly Journal of Economics* 114 (3): 817–68.

Ferber, Marianne, and Julie Nelson, eds. 1993. *Beyond Economic Man: Feminist Theory and Economics.* Chicago: University of Chicago Press.

Ferguson, Ann A. 2001. *Bad Boys: Public Schools in the Making of Black Masculinity.* Ann Arbor: University of Michigan Press.

Ferguson, Ronald F. 1998. "Can Schools Narrow the Test Score Gap?" In Christopher Jencks and Meredith Phillips, eds., *The Black-White Test Score Gap.* Washington, DC: Brookings Institution Press.

———. 2001. "A Diagnostic Analysis of Black-White GPA Disparities in Shaker Heights, Ohio." *Brookings Papers on Education Policy* 2001: 347–414.

Fershtman, Chaim, and Uri Gneezy. 2001. "Discrimination in a Segmented Society: An Experimental Approach." *Quarterly Journal of Economics* 116 (1): 351–77.

Fiore, Michael C. 1992. "Trends in Cigarette Smoking in the United States: The Epidemiology of Tobacco Use." *Medical Clinics of North America* 76 (2): 289–303.

Fisher, Sue. 1995. *Nursing Wounds: Nurse Practitioners, Doctors, Women Patients, and the Negotiation of Meaning.* New Brunswick, NJ: Rutgers University Press.

Fliegel, Seymour. 1993. *Miracle in East Harlem: The Fight for Choice in Public Education.* New York: Random House.

Fogleman, Ronald R. 1995. "The Profession of Arms." *Air Power Journal* 9 (3): 4–5.

Folbre, Nancy. 1994. *Who Pays For the Kids? Gender and the Structures of Constraint.* New York: Routledge.

Foley, Douglas E. 1990. *Learning Capitalist Culture: Deep in the Heart of Texas.* Philadelphia: University of Pennsylvania Press.

———. 2001. "The Great American Football Ritual: Reproducing Race, Class and Gender in Equality." In Andrew Yiannakis and Merrill J. Melnick, eds., *Contemporary Issues in Sociology of Sport.* Champaign, IL: Human Kinetics.

Fordham, Signithia. 1996. *Blacked Out: Dilemmas of Race, Identity and Success at Capital High.* Chicago: University of Chicago Press.

Franke, Katherine M. 1995. "The Central Mistake of Sex Discrimination Law: The Disaggregation of Sex from Gender." *University of Pennsylvania Law Review* 114 (1): 1–99.

Frazier, Franklin. 1957. *The Black Bourgeoisie: The Rise of the New Middle Class in the United States.* New York: Free Press.

Frey, Bruno. 2007. "The Economics of Awards." *European Management Review* 2007 (4): 6–14.

Frey, Bruno S., and Reto Jegen. 2001. "Motivation Crowding Theory." *Journal of Economic Surveys* 15 (5): 589–611.

Friedan, Betty. 1963. *The Feminine Mystique.* New York: W. W. Norton.

Friedman, Milton. 1953. "The Methodology of Positive Economics." In Milton Friedman, *Essays in Positive Economics.* Chicago: University of Chicago Press.

Fryer, Roland G., and Paul Torelli. 2005. "An Empirical Analysis of Acting White." National Bureau of Economic Research, Working Paper 11334. May.

Fudenberg, Drew, and David Levine. 2006. "A Dual-Self Model of Impulse Control." *American Economic Review* 96 (5): 1449–76.

Fulwood, Sam III. 1996. *Waking from the Dream: My Life in the Black Middle Class.* New York: Doubleday.

Gandhi, Mohandas. 1966. *Autobiography.* London: Jonathan Cape.

Gibbons, Robert. 1987. "Piece-Rate Incentive Schemes." *Journal of Labor Economics* 5 (4), part 1, 413–29.

———. "Incentives in Organizations." 1998. *Journal of Economic Perspectives* 12 (4): 115–32.

Gibbons, Robert, and Michael Waldman. 1999. "Careers in Organizations: Theory and Evidence." In Orley Ashenfelter and David Card, eds., *Handbook of Labor Economics.* Amsterdam: Elsevier Science.

Giving USA Foundation. 2008. "U.S. Charitable Giving Estimated to be $307.65 Billion in 2008." www.philanthropy.iupui.edu/News/2009/docs/GivingReaches300billion_06102009.pdf.

Glaeser, Edward L. 2005. "The Political Economy of Hatred." *Quarterly Journal of Economics* 120 (1): 45–86.

Glaeser, Edward L., David I. Laibson, José A. Scheinkman, and Christine L. Soutter. 2000. "Measuring Trust." *Quarterly Journal of Economics* 15 (3): 811–46.

Gneezy, Uri, Muriel Niederle, and Aldo Rustichini. 2003. "Performance in Competitive Environments: Gender Differences." *Quarterly Journal of Economics* 118 (3): 1049–74.

Gneezy, Uri, and Aldo Rustichini. 2000. "A Fine is a Price." *Journal of Legal Studies* 29 (1): 1–18.

Goette, Lorenz, David Huffman, and Stephan Meier. 2006. "The Impact of Group Membership on Cooperation and Norm Enforcement: Evidence Using Random Assignment to Real Social Groups." *American Economic Review* 96 (2): 212–216.

Goffman, Erving. 1959. *The Presentation of Self in Everyday Life.* Garden City, NY: Doubleday.

———. 1961. *Encounters: Two Studies in the Sociology of Interaction.* Indianapolis: Bobbs-Merrill.

Goldin, Claudia. 1990. *Understanding the Gender Gap: An Economic History of American Women.* New York: Oxford University Press.

———. 2006. "The Quiet Revolution that Transformed Women's Employment, Education, and Family." *American Economic Review* 96 (2): 1–21.

Goldin, Claudia, and Lawrence F. Katz. 1997. "Why the United States Led in Education: Lessons from Secondary School Expansion, 1910–1940." National Bureau of Economic Research, Working Paper 6144. August.

Goldman Sachs. n.d. "About Us: The Goldman Sachs Business Principles." http://www2.goldmansachs.com/our-firm/about-us/business-principles .html.

Grant, Gerald. 1988. *The World We Created at Hamilton High.* Cambridge, MA: Harvard University Press.

Greenstein, Theodore N. 1996. "Husbands' Participation in Domestic Labor: Interactive Effects of Wives' and Husbands' Gender Ideologies." *Journal of Marriage and the Family* 58 (3): 585–95.

Hannerz, Ulf. 1969. *Soulside: Inquiries into Ghetto Culture and Community.* New York: Columbia University Press, 1969.

Hanushek, Eric A. 1986. "The Economics of Schooling: Production and Efficiency of Public Schools." *Journal of Economic Literature* 24 (3): 1141–77.

Harris, Judith R. 1998. *The Nurture Assumption: Why Children Turn Out the Way They Do.* New York: Simon and Schuster.

———. 2006. *No Two Alike: Human Nature and Human Individuality.* New York: W. W. Norton.

Haslam, S. Alexander. 2001. *Psychology in Organizations: The Social Identity Approach.* Thousand Oaks, CA: Sage Publications.

Hausman, Daniel. 1992. *The Inexact and Separate Science of Economics.* Cambridge: Cambridge University Press.

Henig, Jeffrey R. 1993. *Rethinking School Choice: Limits of the Market Metaphor.* Princeton, NJ: Princeton University Press.

Heckman, James. 1999. "Policies to Foster Human Capital." National Bureau of Economic Research, Working Paper No. 7288. August.

Hersch, Joni, and Leslie S. Stratton. "Housework, Wages, and the Division of Housework Time for Employed Spouses." *American Economic Review* 84 (2): 120–25.

Hess, Thomas M., Corinne Auman, Stanley J. Colcombe, and Tamara A. Rahhal. 2003. "The Impact of Stereotype Threat on Age Differences in Memory Performance." *Journals of Gerontology Series B: Psychological Sciences and Social Sciences* 58: P3–P11.

Hochschild, Arlie, with Anne Machung. 1990. *The Second Shift.* New York: Avon.

Hodson, Randy. 2001. *Dignity at Work.* Cambridge: Cambridge University Press.

Hoff, Karla, and Priyanka Pandey. 2004. "Belief Systems and Durable Inequalities: An Experimental Investigation of Indian Caste." World Bank, Policy Research Working Paper No. 3351. June.

Hollingshead, August de B. 1949. *Elmtown's Youth: The Impact of Social Classes on Adolescents.* New York: John Wiley.

Holmstrom, Bengt. 1982. "Moral Hazard in Teams." *Bell Journal of Economics* 13 (2): 324–40.

Holmstrom, Bengt, and Paul Milgrom. 1991. "Multitask Principal-Agent Analyses: Incentive Contracts, Asset Ownership, and Job Design." "Papers from the Conference on the New Science of Organization, January 1991," special issue of *Journal of Law, Economics, and Organization* 7:24–52.

Holzer, Harry J., Paul Offner, and Elaine Sorensen. 2004. "Declining Employment among Young Black Less-Educated Men: The Role of Incarceration and Child Support." Institute for Research on Poverty, Discussion Paper 1281–04. May.

Homans, George C. 1951. *The Human Group.* London: Routledge and Kegan Paul.

Honey, Maureen. 1984. *Creating Rosie the Riveter: Class, Gender, and Propaganda during World War II.* Amherst: University of Massachusetts Press.

hooks, bell. 1990. *Yearning: Race, Gender, and Cultural Politics.* Boston: South End Press.

Hopkins, Ann. 2005. "*Price Waterhouse v. Hopkins:* A Personal Account of a Sexual Discrimination Plaintiff." *Hofstra Labor and Employment Law Journal* 22:357–410.

Horst, Ulrich, Alan Kirman, and Miriam Teschl. 2007. "Changing Identity: The Emergence of Social Groups." Institute for Advanced Study, Economics Working Paper 0078, September.

Huck, Steffen, Dorothea Kübler, and Jörgen Weibull. 2003. "Social Norms and Economic Incentives in Firms." Unpublished paper, University College London. May.

Huntington, Samuel P. 1957. *The Soldier and the State: The Theory and Politics of Civil-Military Relations.* Cambridge, MA: Harvard University Press.

Israel, Jared. 2001. "The Sinking of the Ehime Maru: Was U.S. Sub Shadowing the Trawler?" *The Emperor's New Clothes.* March 5. http://emperors-clothes.com/articles/jared/sink.htm.

Jacob, Brian A., and Steven D. Levitt. 2003. "Catching Cheating Teachers: The Results of an Unusual Experiment in Implementing Theory." *Brookings-Wharton Papers on Urban Affairs* 2003:185–209.

Janowitz, Morris. 1960. *The Professional Soldier: A Social and Political Portrait.* New York: Free Press, 1960.

Jencks, Christopher, and Meredith Phillips. 1998. *The Black-White Test Score Gap.* Washington, DC: Brookings Institution Press.

Juravich, Tom. C. 1985. *Chaos on the Shop Floor: A Worker's View of Quality, Production and Management.* Philadelphia: Temple University Press.

Kandori, Michihiro. 1992. "Social Norms and Community Enforcement." *Review of Economic Studies* 59 (1): 63–80.

Kanter, Rosabeth Moss. 1977. *Men and Women of the Corporation.* New York: Basic Books.

Kaufman, Phillip, Martha N. Alt, and Christopher Chapman. 2004. *Dropout Rates in the United States: 2001* (NCES 2005046). U.S. Department of Education, National Center for Education Statistics. Washington, DC: U.S. Government Printing Office.

Keegan, John. 1976. *The Face of Battle.* New York: Viking Press.

Keynes, John Maynard. 1960. *The General Theory of Employment, Interest and Money.* New York: Harcourt, Brace and Company.

Kling, Jeffrey R. 2006. "Incarceration Length, Employment and Earnings." *American Economic Review* 96 (3): 863–76.

Kogut, Bruce, and Udo Zander. 1996. "What Firms Do? Coordination, Identity and Learning." *Organization Science* 7 (5): 502–18.

Krug, Edward A. 1964. *The Shaping of the American High School, 1880–1920.* Madison: University of Wisconsin Press.

———. 1972. *The Shaping of the American High School, 1920–1941.* Madison: University of Wisconsin Press.

Kuran, Timur, and William H. Sandholm. 2008. "Cultural Integration and Its Discontents." *Review of Economic Studies* 75 (1): 201–28.

Laibson, David I. 1997. "Golden Eggs and Hyperbolic Discounting." "In Memory of Amos Tversky (1937–1996)," special issue of *Quarterly Journal of Economics* 112 (2): 443–77.

Laibson, David I., Andrea Repetto, and Jeremy Tobacman. 1998. "Self-Control and Saving for Retirement." *Brookings Papers on Economic Activity* 1998 (1): 91–172.

Lazear, Edward P. 1989. "Pay Equality and Industrial Politics." *Journal of Political Economy* 97 (3): 561–80.

Lazear, Edward P., and Sherwin Rosen. 1990. "Male-Female Wage Differentials in Job Ladders." *Journal of Labor Economics* 8 (1), part 2, S106–S123.

Levitt, Steven D., and Sudhir A. Venkatesh. 2000. "An Economic Analysis of a Drug-Selling Gang's Finances." *Quarterly Journal of Economics* 115 (3): 755–89.

Lindbeck, Assar, Sten Nyberg, and Jorgen W. Weibull. 1999. "Social Norms and Economic Incentives in the Welfare State." *Quarterly Journal of Economics* 114 (1): 1–35.

———. 2003. "Social Norms and Welfare State Dynamics." *Journal of the European Economic Association* 1 (2–3): 533–42.

Lipsky, David. 2003. *Absolutely American: Four Years at West Point.* Boston: Houghton Mifflin.

Loewenstein, George. 1987. "Anticipation and the Valuation of Delayed Consumption." *Economic Journal* 97 (387): 666–84.

Loewenstein, George, and Drazen Prelec. 1992. "Anomalies in Intertemporal Choice: Evidence and an Interpretation." *Quarterly Journal of Economics* 107 (2): 573–97.

Loewenstein, George, and Richard H. Thaler. 1989. "Anomalies: Intertemporal Choice." *Journal of Economic Perspectives* 3 (4): 181–93.

Loury, Glenn C. 1995. *One by One from the Inside Out.* New York: Free Press.

———. 2002. *The Anatomy of Racial Inequality.* Cambridge, MA: Harvard University Press.

Lundberg, Shelly, and Robert Pollak. 1993. "Separate Spheres Bargaining and the Marriage Market." *Journal of Political Economy* 101 (6): 988–1010.

Mackie, Gerry. 1996. "Ending Footbinding and Infibulation: A Convention Account." *American Sociological Review* 61 (6): 999–1017.

MacKinnon, Catharine A. 1979. *Sexual Harassment of Working Women.* New Haven, CT: Yale University Press.

Manski, Charles F. 1993. "Identification of Endogenous Social Effects: The Reflection Problem." *Review of Economic Studies* 60 (3): 531–42.

Martin J. A., B. E. Hamilton, P. D. Sutto, S. J. Ventura, F. Menacker, S. Kirmeyer, and M. L. Munson. 2007. *Births: Final Data for 2005.* National Vital Statistics Reports 56, no 6. Hyattsville, MD: National Center for Health Statistics. www.cdc.gov/nchs/data/nvsr/nvsr56/nvsr56_06.pdf.

McLeish, Kendra N., and Robert J. Oxoby. 2006. "Identity, Cooperation, and Punishment." Unpublished paper, University of Calgary. March.

McNally, Jeffrey A. 1991. *The Adult Development of Career Army Officers.* New York: Praeger.

Meier, Deborah. 1995. *The Power of Their Ideas.* Boston: Beacon Press.

Miguel, Edward, and Mary Kay Gugerty. 2005. "Ethnic Diversity, Social

Sanctions, and Public Goods in Kenya." *Journal of Public Economics* 89 (11–12): 2325–68.

Milgrom, Paul, and John Roberts. 1992. *Economics, Organization and Management.* Englewood Cliffs, NJ: Prentice-Hall.

Milkman, Ruth. 1987. *Gender at Work: The Dynamics of Job Segregation by Sex during World War II.* Urbana: University of Illinois Press.

Miller, Kerby A. 1985. "Assimilation and Alienation: Irish Emigrants' Responses to Industrial America." In P. J. Drudy, ed., *The Irish in America: Emigration, Assimilation and Impact.* Cambridge: Cambridge University Press.

Mincer, Jacob, and Solomon Polachek. 1974. "Family Investments in Human Capital: Earnings of Women." *Journal of Political Economy* 82 (2), part 2, S76–S108.

Moore, Harold G., and Joseph L. Galloway. 1992. *We Were Soldiers Once—and Young: Ia Drang, the Battle That Changed the War in Vietnam.* New York: Random House.

Moskos, Charles C., John Allen Williams, and David R. Segal. 2000. "Armed Forces after the Cold War." In Charles C. Moskos, John Allen Williams, and David R. Segal, eds., *Armed Forces after the Cold War.* Oxford: Oxford University Press.

Mullainathan, Sendhil, and Andrei Shleifer. 2005. "The Market for News." *American Economic Review* 95 (4): 1031–53.

Munnell, Alicia H., Geoffrey M. B. Tootell, Lynn E. Browne, and James McEneaney. 1996. "Mortgage Lending in Boston: Interpreting HMDA Data." *American Economic Review* 86 (1): 25–53.

Myrdal, Gunnar. 1944. *An American Dilemma: The Negro Problem and American Democracy.* New York: Harper.

Nash, John. 1953. "Two-Person Cooperative Games." *Econometrica* 21 (1): 128–40.

Nation of Islam. n.d. "What the Muslims Want." www.noi.org/muslim_program.htm.

Neal, Derek. 1997. "The Effects of Catholic Secondary Schooling on Educational Achievement." *Journal of Labor Economics* 15 (1), part 1, 98–123.

———. 2005. "Black-White Labour Market Inequality in the United States." Draft paper for *New Palgrave Dictionary of Economics.*

———. 2006. "Why Has Black-White Skill Convergence Stopped?" In Eric A. Hanushek and Finis Welch, eds., *Handbook of the Economics of Education.* Vol.1. Amsterdam: North-Holland.

Nelson, Jill. 1993. *Volunteer Slavery: An Authentic Negro Experience.* New York: Penguin.

Newman, Katherine B. 2000. *No Shame in My Game: The Working Poor in the Inner City.* New York: Vintage.

NIAOnline. 2005. "When Keeping It Real Goes Right." August 30. www.niaonline.com.

Nisbett, Richard E., and Dov Cohen. 1996. *Culture of Honor: The Psychology of Violence in the South*. Boulder, CO: Westview Press.

Norton, Anne. 1988. *Reflections on Political Identity*. Baltimore, MD: Johns Hopkins University Press.

Ogbu, John U. 1974. *The Next Generation: An Ethnography of Education in an Urban Neighborhood*. New York: Academic Press.

Ostrom, Elinor. 1990. *Governing the Commons: The Evolution of Institutions for Collective Action*. Cambridge: Cambridge University Press.

Oxoby, Robert J. 2004. "Cognitive Dissonance, Status and Growth of the Underclass." *Economic Journal* 114 (498): 727–49.

Padavic, Irene. 1991. "The Re-creation of Gender in a Male Workplace." *Symbolic Interaction* 14 (3): 279–94.

Parker Core Knowledge School. n.d. "Dress Code." *PCKS Parent Handbook*. www.ckcs.net.

Pepper, John. 2005. *What Really Matters*. Cincinnati, OH: Procter and Gamble.

Peshkin, Allen. 1986. *God's Choice: The Total World of a Fundamentalist Christian School*. Chicago: University of Chicago Press.

Peters, Thomas J., and Robert H. Waterman Jr. 1982. *In Search of Excellence*. New York: Harper and Row.

Phelps, Edmund S., and Robert A. Pollak. 1968. "On Second-Best National Saving and Game-Equilibrium Growth." *Review of Economic Studies* 35 (2): 185–99.

Pierce, Jennifer. 1995. *Gender Trials: Emotional Lives in Contemporary Law Firms*. Berkeley: University of California Press.

Pierson, Ruth R. 1986. *They're Still Women After All: The Second World War and Canadian Womanhood*. Toronto: McClelland and Stewart.

Powell, Arthur G., Eleanor Farrar, and David K. Cohen. 1985. *The Shopping Mall High School: Winners and Losers in the Educational Marketplace*. Boston: Houghton Mifflin.

Prendergast, Canice. 1999. "The Provision of Incentives in Firms." *Journal of Economic Literature* 37 (1): 7–63.

———. 2003. "The Motivation and Bias of Bureaucrats." Unpublished paper, Graduate School of Business, University of Chicago. October.

Preston, Anne. 1997. "Sex, Kids, and Commitment to the Workplace: Employers, Employees, and the Mommy Track." Russell Sage Foundation, Working Paper No. 123.

Price Waterhouse v. Hopkins. 1989. No. 87–1167, 490 U.S. 228; 109 S. Ct. 1775; 104 L. Ed. 2d 268; 1989 U.S. LEXIS 2230; 57 U.S.L.W. 4469; 49 Fair Empl. Prac. Cas. (BNA) 954; 49 Empl. Prac. Dec. (CCH) P38,936. October 31, 1988, Argued. May 1, 1989, Decided. http://bss.sfsu.edu/naff/Diversity/fall%202001/Hopkins%20v%20PW.htm.

Pringle, Rosemary. 1988. *Secretaries Talk: Sexuality, Power and Work*. New York: Verso.

Rabin, Matthew. 1993. "Incorporating Fairness into Game Theory and Economics." *American Economic Review* 83 (5): 1281–1302.

Rainwater, Lee. 1970. *Behind Ghetto Walls: Black Families in a Federal Slum.* Chicago: Aldine, 1970.

Ravitch, Diane. 1983. *The Troubled Crusade: American Education, 1945–1980.* New York: Basic Books.

Ricks, Thomas E. 1997. "The Widening Gap between the Military and Society." *Atlantic Monthly,* July, 66–78.

Rivkin, Steven G., Eric A. Hanushek, and John F. Kain. 2005. "Teachers, Schools, and Academic Achievement." *Econometrica* 73 (2): 417–58.

Rob, Rafael, and Peter Zemsky. 2002. "Social Capital, Corporate Culture, and Incentive Intensity." *RAND Journal of Economics* 33 (2): 243–57.

Rodgers, William. 1969. *Think: A Biography of the Watsons and IBM.* New York: Stein and Day.

Rodriguez, Richard. 1982. *Hunger of Memory: The Education of Richard Rodriguez.* New York: Bantam.

Romer, Paul M. 1994. "Preferences, Promises, and the Politics of Enlightenment." Unpublished paper, University of California at Berkeley. December.

Rostker, Bernard, Harry Thie, James Lacy, Jennifer Kawata, and Susanna Purcell. 1993. *The Defense Officer Personnel Management Act of 1980: A Retrospective Assessment.* Santa Monica, CA: RAND.

Roy, Donald F. 1952. "Quota Restriction and Goldbricking in a Machine Shop." *American Journal of Sociology* 57 (5): 427–42.

———. 1953. "Work Satisfaction and Social Reward in Quota Achievement: An Analysis of Piecework Incentive." *American Sociological Review* 18 (5): 507–14.

Rumbaut, Rubén G. 2000. "Children of Immigrants and Their Achievement: The Role of Family, Acculturation, Social Class, Gender, Ethnicity, and School Contexts." Unpublished paper, Michigan State University.

Rumsfeld, Donald H. 2002. "Lucky Us: A Tribute to Milton Friedman," *National Review On-line.* July 31. www.nationalreview.com/nrof_document/documento73102.asp.

Said, Edward W. 1978. *Orientalism.* New York: Random House.

Schelling, Thomas C. 1971. "Dynamic Models of Segregation." *Journal of Mathematical Sociology* 1 (1): 143–86.

Schultz, Vicki. 1998. "Reconceptualizing Sexual Harassment." *Yale Law Journal* 107 (6): 1683–1805.

———. 2003. "The Sanitized Workplace." *Yale Law Journal* 112 (8): 2061–2193.

Seashore, Stanley E. 1954. *Group Cohesiveness in the Industrial Work Group.* Ann Arbor, MI: Institute for Social Research, Survey Research Center.

Selznick, Philip. 1957. *Leadership in Administration.* Berkeley: University of California Press.

Sen, Amartya K. 1970. "The Impossibility of a Paretian Liberal." *Journal of Political Economy* 78 (1): 152–57.

———. 1977. "Rational Fools: A Critique of the Behavioral Foundations of Economic Theory." *Philosophy and Public Affairs* 6 (4): 317–44.

———. 1985. "Goals, Commitment and Identity." *Journal of Law, Economics, and Organization* 1 (2): 341–55.

———. 1997. "Maximization and the Act of Choice." *Econometrica* 65 (4): 745–79.

———. 2006. *Identity and Violence: The Illusion of Destiny.* New York: W. W. Norton.

Shapiro, Carl, and Joseph E. Stiglitz. 1984. "Equilibrium Unemployment as a Worker Discipline Device." *American Economic Review* 74 (3): 433–44.

Sherif, Muzafer, O. J. Harvey, B. Jack White, William R. Hood, and Carolyn W. Sherif. 1954. *Intergroup Conflict and Cooperation: The Robbers Cave Experiment.* Norman, OK: University Book Exchange.

Smith, Vicki. 2001. *Crossing the Great Divide: Worker Risk and Opportunity in the New Economy.* Ithaca, NY: ILR Press.

Spencer, Steven M., Claude M. Steele, and Diane M. Quinn. 1999. "Stereotype Threat and Women's Math Performance." *Journal of Experimental Social Psychology* 35 (1): 4–28.

Stamberg, Susan. 2001. "Profile: Loyalty in the Military." Interview. National Public Radio. March 27.

Stanley, Marcus, Lawrence Katz, and Alan Krueger. 1998. "Impacts of Employment Programs: The American Experience." Unpublished paper, Harvard University.

Staples, Brent. 1994. *Parallel Time: Growing Up in Black and White.* New York: Pantheon.

Steele, Claude, and Joshua Aronson. 1995. "Stereotype Threat and the Intellectual Test Performance of African Americans," *Journal of Personality and Social Psychology* 69 (5): 797–811.

Stewart, James B. 1997. "NEA Presidential Address, 1994: Toward Broader Involvement of Black Economists in Discussions of Race and Public Policy: A Plea for a Reconceptualization of Race and Power in Economic Theory." In James B. Stewart, ed., *African Americans and Post-Industrial Labor Markets.* New Brunswick, NJ: Transactions Publishers.

Stigler, George J., and Gary S. Becker. 1977. "De Gustibus Non Est Disputandum." *American Economic Review* 67 (1): 76–90.

Stouffer, Samuel A., Edward A. Suchman, Leland C. DeVinney, Shirley A. Star, and Robin M. Williams Jr. 1949a. *The American Soldier.* Vol. 1. *Adjustment during Army Life.* Princeton, NJ: Princeton University Press.

Stouffer, Samuel A., Arthur A. Lumsdaine, Marion Harper Lumsdaine, Robin M. Williams Jr., M. Brewster Smith, Irving L. Janis, Shirley A. Star, and Leonard S. Cottrell Jr. 1949b. *The American Soldier*. Vol. 2. *Combat and Its Aftermath*. Princeton, NJ: Princeton University Press.

Strober, Myra H., and Carolyn Arnold. 1987. "The Dynamics of Occupational Segregation among Bank Tellers." In Clair Brown and Joseph Pechman, eds., *Gender in the Workplace*. Washington, DC: Brookings Institution Press.

Strotz, Robert H. 1956. "Myopia and Inconsistency in Dynamic Utility Maximization." *Review of Economic Studies* 23 (3): 165–80.

Tajfel, Henri, Michael G. Billig, Robert P. Bundy, and Claude Flament. 1971. "Social Categorization and Intergroup Behavior." *European Journal of Social Psychology* 1 (2): 149–78.

Terkel, Studs. 1974. *Working: People Talk About What They Do All Day and How They Feel About What They Do*. New York: Pantheon.

"Text of Obama's Speech: A More Perfect Union." 2008. *Wall Street Journal*. March 18. http://blogs.wsj.com/washwire/2008/03/18/text-of-obamas-speech-a-more-perfect-union/.

Thaler, Richard H., and Hersh M. Shefrin. 1981. "An Economic Theory of Self-Control." *Journal of Political Economy* 89 (2): 392–406.

TobaccoDocuments.Org. n.d. "Tobacco Documents Online: Collections—PM Advertising Archive." http://tobaccodocuments.org/ads_pm/.

Tolnay, Stewart E., Glenn Deane, and E. M. Beck. 1996. "Vicarious Violence: Spatial Effects on Southern Lynchings, 1890–1919." *American Journal of Sociology* 102 (3): 788–815.

Tsuya, Noriko O., Larry L. Bumpass, and Minja Kim Choe. 2000. "Gender, Employment, and Housework in Japan, South Korea, and the United States." *Review of Population and Social Policy* 9:195–220.

Turner, Victor Witter. 1995. *The Ritual Process*. New York: Aldine de Gruyter.

U.S. Bureau of the Census. 1992. *Statistical Abstract of the United States*. Washington, DC: U. S. Government Printing Office.

———. 2000. *Statistical Abstract of the United States*. www.census.gov/prod/2001pubs/statab/sec13.pdf.

———. 2006. *Statistical Abstract of the United States*. www.census.gov/prod/2005pubs/06statab/vitstat.pdf.

———. 2008. *Current Population Survey: Annual Social and Economic Supplement, 2007*. www.census.gov/macro/032008/pov/new03_100_06.htm.

———. 2009. *Statistical Abstract of the United States*. Washington, DC: U.S. Government Printing Office.

U.S. Census. 2008. *Current Population Survey, Annual Social and Economic (ASEC) Supplement*. http://pubdb3.census.gov/macro/032008/pov/new03_100_06.htm.

U.S. Census Bureau. n.d. *Historical Poverty Tables*. www.census.gov/hhes/www/poverty/histpov/hstpov2.html.

———. 2003. "Women Edge Men in High School Diplomas, Breaking 13-

Year Deadlock." *U.S. Census Bureau News.* March 21. www.census.gov/
Press-Release/www/releases/archives/education/000818.html.

U.S. Census Bureau and U.S. Bureau of Labor Statistics. 2008. *Current Population Survey.* www.bls.gov/cps/cpsaat11.pdf.

U.S. Court of Appeals for the Eighth Circuit. 1997. *Lois E. Jenson v. Eveleth Taconite Co.* Case 97–1147. www.ca8.uscourts.gov/opndir/97/12/971147P.pdf.

U.S. Department of Labor. n.d. *Find It! By Topic: Training–Job Corps.* www.dol.gov/dol/topic/training/jobcorps.htm.

———. 1968. *Job Tenure of Workers, January 1968.* Special Labor Force Report 112. Washington, DC: U.S. Government Printing Office.

U.S. Department of Labor, Bureau of Labor Statistics. 2006. *Current Population Survey: Annual Demographic Survey, March Supplement.* http://pubdb3.census.gov/macro/032005/pov/new01_200_05.htm.

U.S. Military Academy at West Point. n.d. "About the Academy." www.usma.edu/about.asp.

———. n.d. "U.S. Military Academy Mission." www.usma.edu/mission.asp.

Valenzuela, Angela. 1999. *Subtractive Schooling: U.S.-Mexican Youth and the Politics of Caring.* Albany: State University of New York Press.

Varian, Hal. 1974. "Equity, Envy, and Efficiency." *Journal of Economic Theory* 9 (1): 63–91.

Wakin, Malham. n.d. "Service before Self." In United States Air Force, *Guides, Essays and Articles about the Air Force Core Values.* www.usafa.af.mil/core-value/service-before-self.html.

Waldron, Ingrid. 1991. "Patterns and Causes of Gender Differences in Smoking." *Journal of Social Science and Medicine* 32 (9): 989–1005.

Watson, James D. 1969. *The Double Helix: A Personal Account of the Discovery of the Structure of DNA.* New York: New American Library.

Watson, James D., and Francis H. C. Crick. 1953. "A Structure for Deoxyribose Nucleic Acid." *Nature* 171 (4356): 737–38.

Weber, Max. 1978 [1914]. *Economy and Society: An Outline of Interpretive Sociology.* Vol. 2. Ed. Guenther Roth and Claus Wittich. Berkeley: University of California Press.

Weiss, Lois. 1990. *Working Class without Work: High School Students in a De-industrializing Economy.* New York: Routledge.

Whyte, William Foote. 1943. *Street Corner Society: The Social Structure of an Italian Slum.* Chicago: University of Chicago Press.

Williams, Christine. 1989. *Gender Differences at Work: Women and Men in Nontraditional Occupations.* Berkeley: University of California Press, 1989.

Willis, Paul R. 1977. *Learning to Labour: How Working Class Kids Get Working Class Jobs.* Westmead, U.K.: Saxon House.

Wilson, William J. 1987. *The Truly Disadvantaged.* Chicago: University of Chicago Press.

————. 1996. *When Work Disappears: The World of the New Urban Poor.* New York: Knopf.

Wurzburg, Lynne A., and Robert A. Klonoff. 1997. "Legal Approaches to Sex Discrimination." In Hope Landrine and Elizabeth A. Klonoff, eds., *Discrimination against Women: Prevalence, Consequences, Remedies.* Thousand Oaks, CA: Sage Publications.

Young, Peyton. 2008. "Self-Perception and Self-Knowledge." Department of Economics, University of Oxford, Working Paper No. 383.

"You've Come a Long Way, Baby." n.d. Tobacco Ads Online. http://tobaccodocuments.org/ads_pm/2058502462.html.

Index

Waterman, Robert H., Jr., 49, 141n35
Watson, James, 116, 119, 150n4,6
Watson, Thomas, 49
Weaver, Robert, 136n13
Weber, Max, 58, 59, 142n61
Weibull, Jörgen, 137n5, 139n10
Weiss, Lois, 68, 143n19
welfare, utility and, 23
Western Electric Company, 48, 54
West Point. *See* United States Military Academy at West Point
"When Keeping It Real Goes Right" (*NiaOnline*), 102
When Work Disappears (Wilson), 104
White, B. Jack, 28, 137n1
Whitehead, John, 5, 59
Whyte, William Foote, 101, 149n20
Williams, Christine, 145n4, 146n12
Williams, John Allen, 45, 140n20
Williams, Robin M., Jr., 141n26,27, 142n55,58,59
Willis, Paul R., 64–65, 68, 72, 101, 122, 143n14,19, 149n21
Wilson, Timothy D., 140n15
Wilson, William Julius, 101, 104, 149n18
women. *See* gender
Women's Movement, 20, 90, 114, 146n16
work and gender, 83–96, 127, 145–48n1–39; in the home,

92–94, 95, 147–48n35,36; identity model of, 86–88; job tags, 84–85, 90, 95, 118; job tenure, 90, 146n17; the law on, 91–92; new conclusions, 88–91; occupational segregation, 83–86, 88, 89, 90–91, 146n15; theory and evidence, 88; wages and, 87, 88–89
work and race. *See* minority poverty
workgroups: in the civilian workplace, 52–56, 58; in the military, 46, 56–57
work incentives, 14–15, 39–59, 118, 138–42n1–62; identity model of, 41–43; shared goals as, 58–59; traditional economics on, 40–41. *See also* civilian workplace; military; monetary incentives
World War II, 46, 85
World We Created at Hamilton High, The (Grant), 62–64, 117
Wright, Jeremiah, 107–8
Wright, Richard, 100
Wurzburg, Lynne A., 147n27

Yale University, 49
Yellen, Janet L., 139n5
Young, Peyton, 34, 138n28

Zame, William, 137n7
Zander, Udo, 139n8
Zemsky, Peter, 137n5